Based in Somerset, Jane Tib... having been a teacher and he... ministry in 1999. She has a wide experience of primary school teaching and has taught music and drama in secondary schools. She was also the head of a multinational school in Saudi Arabia and has worked in the Falklands. Since leaving teaching, she has continued to be involved with schools as a governor and as a SIAS inspector.

Training has played a key role in Jane's work over recent years, with the provision of training courses for people who work with children in the predominantly voluntary sector of education. She has contributed to education courses for clergy and ministers-in-training. She is also an accredited Godly Play teacher. Jane runs a variety of workshops in churches and schools and has experience of the planning and leading of festivals and large events. Her workshops are lively and interactive. She also leads an annual holiday club and summer camp for children.

As a writer, Jane has compiled a number of resources for churches and schools to support the church's year from Advent to All Souls. She also contributes to *ROOTS* magazine and produces 'Young Church Mag', the weekly puzzle sheet for children, and 'SundayMax', a weekly online resource. Jane's first book for Barnabas for Children, *Creative Ideas for Advent and Christmas*, was published in 2011.

Barnabas for Children

Barnabas for Children® is a registered word mark and the logo is a registered device mark of The Bible Reading Fellowship.

Text copyright © Jane Tibbs 2014
Illustrations copyright © Mary Hall 2014
The author asserts the moral right
to be identified as the author of this work

Published by
The Bible Reading Fellowship
15 The Chambers, Vineyard
Abingdon OX14 3FE
United Kingdom
Tel: +44 (0)1865 319700
Email: enquiries@brf.org.uk
Website: www.brf.org.uk
BRF is a Registered Charity

ISBN 978 0 85746 245 9
First published 2014
10 9 8 7 6 5 4 3 2 1 0
All rights reserved

Acknowledgements
Unless otherwise stated, scripture quotations are taken from the Contemporary English Version of the Bible published by HarperCollins Publishers, copyright © 1991, 1992, 1995 American Bible Society.

Scripture quotations taken from the Holy Bible, New International Version, copyright © 1973, 1978, 1984 by International Bible Society, are used by permission of Hodder & Stoughton Publishers, a member of the Hachette Livre Group UK. All rights reserved. 'NIV' is a registered trademark of International Bible Society. UK trademark number 1448790.

Cover photos: top left to right: © Dave White/iStock/Thinkstock; © schmaelterphoto/ iStock/Thinkstock; © Teenoo/iStock/Thinkstock; bottom left to right: © Fernow/ F1online/Thinkstock; © Rebecca Dickerson/iStock/Thinkstock; © Hemant Mehta/ IndiaPicture/Thinkstock; butterflies © miriam-doerr/iStock/Thinkstock; chocolate eggs © GOSPHOTODESIGN/iStock/Thinkstock

Every effort has been made to trace and contact copyright owners for material used in this resource. We apologise for any inadvertent omissions or errors, and would ask those concerned to contact us so that full acknowledgement can be made in the future.

A catalogue record for this book is available from the British Library

Printed and bound by CPI Group (UK) Ltd, Croydon CR0 4YY

Creative Ideas for
Lent & Easter

80 seasonal activities for use with children

Jane Tibbs

To Juzz and Tim, who have always been willing guinea pigs.

Acknowledgements

Thank you to all those who relentlessly continue to follow my instructions and discover if the ideas really work.

Photocopy permission

Contents

Appendix 2: Templates

Foreword

In a world that thinks more about Easter bunnies and chocolate than the real significance of Easter, *Creative Ideas for Lent and Easter* offers us the opportunity to explore the events before, during and after the festival of Easter.

Jane Tibbs has written a book that responds to the preparations for and celebration of this most important Christian festival, with ideas including the party time before Ash Wednesday, Lent, Mothering Sunday, Palm Sunday, Holy Week, Easter and the six weeks following to Rogationtide and Ascension Day. It is packed with creativity that can be used in a variety of situations—at home, at school, in church and in the community.

The weeks surrounding Easter are spiritually rich and this time of year has the potential to engage not only children and their families but whole communities in the key events of their faith. Here is a collection of possibilities for communities as well as church to engage with, providing opportunities for those who think that the message of Easter needs to be heard more widely and its truth experienced more fully by all who are made in the image of God.

No one who turns these pages could fail to enjoy the fun of establishing traditions, old and new, that will make the Easter story come alive.

The Right Revd Peter Maurice
Bishop of Taunton

Introduction

The 40 days leading up to the great feast of Easter are an ideal time to get not only children and young people engaged in their faith but whole communities as well. As we make our journey through Lent towards the joy of Easter, there are so many things we can do to bring this special time alive.

How to use this book

This book contains a huge variety of ideas and activities that could be used at home, in schools or in church services or groups. Some of the activities focus very much on the meaning of Lent while others look at the wonderful feast of Easter and the continuing celebrations that lead us through the season of Easter to Ascension Day.

Don't think you need to try everything the first time you use this book. There are enough ideas to last for several seasons.

Interesting facts about Lent and Eastertide

Shrovetide

In many parts of the world, the days before Lent begins are a time of revelry and merrymaking. This festive time is called 'Carnival', which comes from the Latin words that mean 'a farewell to meat' (during Lent, the early Christians gave up meat and other rich foods). The final day of Carnival is Shrove Tuesday, a day when celebrations come to an end and Christians confess their sins ('shrive' themselves) in preparation for Lent.

The four days leading up to Lent are also described as Shrovetide. The old names for these days are:

- Egg Saturday, or Shrove Saturday.
- Quinquagesima Sunday, or Shrove Sunday, which is the 50th day before Easter.
- Collop Monday, or Shrove Monday, which is named after the traditional dish of the day—collops of bacon served with eggs. A collop is a chunk or slice of meat and the fat from these slices was used to cook the following day's pancakes.
- Pancake Day, or Shrove Tuesday.

When Lent was observed more rigorously than it is now, Shrovetide was celebrated with games, sports, dancing and revelries. There were feasts to use up the food that could not be eaten during the Lenten fast. Football was played in the streets and Nickanan Night (as Shrove Monday was called in Cornwall) was an opportunity for boys to run riot in the villages, hiding gates, taking off door knockers and making off with anything that householders had forgotten to put away.

Lent

Lent is a time when Christians remember the 40 days and nights that Jesus spent alone in the desert without food and being tempted by the devil. Jesus used this time to prepare for his work by fasting and praying. Luke's Gospel says, 'Jesus, full of the Holy Spirit, returned from the Jordan and was led by the Spirit in the desert, where for forty days he was tempted by the devil. He ate nothing during those days, and at the end of them he was hungry' (Luke 4:1–2, NIV). So, as in the Bible, Christians spend 40 days in preparing themselves to rejoice at the resurrection of Jesus Christ at Easter.

The number 40 is a special number in the Bible. It signifies preparation for something special:

- The rain lasted for 40 days in the mighty flood (Genesis 7:17).
- Moses stayed on Mount Sinai for 40 days (Exodus 24:18).

- Jonah gave the people of Nineveh 40 days to repent (Jonah 3:4).
- Jesus, before starting his ministry, spent 40 days in the desert in prayer and fasting (Luke 4:2).

The season of Lent includes the 40 days from Ash Wednesday to Easter Day. The official observance of Lent does not include Sundays because Christians are meant to celebrate every Sunday as a 'little Easter'.

In the early days of the church, Lent was a time of fasting, strict self-discipline and examination of how one was living. In fact, by the Middle Ages, there were so many rules and regulations about observing Lent that some people actually dreaded the season. Today those rules have relaxed considerably. For many people, however, Lent is still a time to reflect on their relationship with God, to spend more time in Bible reading and prayer, and to find ways of serving others.

Mothering Sunday is the fourth Sunday in Lent. Traditionally it was a day when people could take a break from the seriousness of Lent. The tradition of calling this day Mothering Sunday goes back to Roman times when, as the Christian church spread, there developed the pattern of honouring the church as a mother figure. From this developed the tradition of children honouring their mothers. Youngsters who worked away from home were allowed to go and visit their mothers on Mothering Sunday, and they may have taken a Simnel cake as a gift.

The feast of the Annunciation to the Blessed Virgin Mary is celebrated on 25 March. This festival marks the visit of the angel Gabriel to Mary, during which he told her that she would be the mother of Jesus. As Easter is a 'movable feast' (see pages 12–13), if 25 March happens to fall in Holy Week, in Easter Week or on a Sunday, the Annunciation is celebrated a week after Easter.

A week before Easter, the arrival of Palm Sunday marks the beginning of Holy Week. These final days of Lent are the most sacred time in the Christian church year. For many churches and families, Holy Week is a time of intense reflection and prayer as people remember the sacrifice that Jesus made.

Wednesday in Holy Week is known as Spy Wednesday because on this day Judas made a bargain with the high priest to betray Jesus for 30 silver pieces (Matthew 26:14–16; Mark 14:10–11; Luke 22:1–6). In Poland, the young people throw an effigy of Judas from the top of a church steeple. Then it is dragged through the village amid hurling sticks and stones. What remains of the effigy is drowned in a nearby stream or pond.

Thursday in Holy Week is known as Maundy Thursday. The word 'Maundy' comes from the Latin word *mandatum* which means 'commandment'. On the Thursday of Holy Week, Jesus gave his disciples a 'new' commandment—to love one another (John 13:34).

Of course, Friday is Good Friday, when Christians throughout the world gather to remember the day of Jesus' death.

Easter

On Easter Day, the mood suddenly changes to one of great joy as Christians around the world celebrate Christ's victory over death and the new life he promises to those who follow him. On the first Easter morning, Jesus' friends, Mary Magdalene, Mary the mother of James and Salome, went to the tomb to anoint Jesus' body but found that the stone blocking the tomb had been rolled away and his body was not there. They saw an angel in the tomb who said that Jesus had risen from the dead and told them to go and tell the disciples the amazing news. They went and told the disciples and Peter immediately rushed off to the tomb. He, too, was amazed at what he saw. At first the disciples were confused and some of them didn't believe it, but soon they saw Jesus for themselves.

The first person to see the risen Jesus was Mary Magdalene. She was crying in the garden when she saw a man who she thought was the gardener. The man said to her, 'Why are you crying?' She replied to him, 'If you have carried him away, please tell me where you have put him, and I will get him.' Jesus said, 'Mary!' and Mary immediately recognised his voice (John 20:10–16).

For Christians, the dawn of Easter Day, with its message of new life, is the high point of the Christian year. It recalls Jesus overcoming sin and death and gives Christians the promise of hope for the kingdom. For Christians, Jesus was the perfect sinless man, so when he died on the cross he became a perfect sacrifice in the Jewish tradition. Then, to prove that there is life after death, Jesus rose from the dead on the third day, as he'd said he would.

Easter is the oldest celebrated season in the Christian church year—even older than Christmas. It is celebrated from Easter Sunday until Pentecost, 50 days later. Pentecost was the day when God's Holy Spirit filled Jesus' followers and inspired them to tell the world about their faith. Christians observe Pentecost as the end of the Easter season and the official 'birthday' of the Christian Church.

The Easter season includes Rogationtide and the feast of the Ascension. Rogation Sunday is the sixth Sunday of Easter and is so called because of the words in the Prayer Book Gospel reading for the day: 'Whatever you ask the Father in my name, he will give to you.' The Latin for 'ask' is *rogare*, and the word developed to become Rogation Sunday. It is a traditional time for villages to get together to bless their crops and pray (or ask) for a good harvest.

The Monday, Tuesday and Wednesday after Rogation Sunday are also called Rogation Days and lead to Ascension Day, which is always celebrated on a Thursday. On Ascension Day we celebrate Jesus' return to heaven and his promise to send the Holy Spirit to help us for ever.

Easter is a movable feast, which means that the date changes from year to year. Easter can fall on any date from 22 March to 25 April. The reason for this is that Easter is based on the lunar calendar rather than our more well-known solar calendar. Easter always falls on the first Sunday following the full moon (the Paschal full moon) after 21 March. If the full moon falls on a Sunday, then Easter Day is the next Sunday.

The date of Easter Day

- 2015: 5 April
- 2016: 27 March
- 2017: 16 April
- 2018: 1 April
- 2019: 21 April
- 2020: 12 April

✣

Creative ideas for the preparation for Lent

Pancake party

Shrove Tuesday is an ideal opportunity to have a party.

Start by briefly explaining some of the background to Shrove Tuesday. No one really knows how long people have been making pancakes. They may be similar to the flatbread made more than 12,000 years ago. We can only suppose that families had as much fun making their pancakes then as we do today.

Shrove Tuesday (Pancake Day) is the last day before the start of Lent. Years ago, great feasts would have been held to use up supplies of fat, butter and eggs, as people were not allowed to eat these foods during Lent. People gave them up as a reminder of the time Jesus spent in the wilderness before he began his ministry. For 40 days Jesus prayed and fasted and was tempted by the devil.

Lent is a period of 40 days, not counting the Sundays. With the Sundays, it is actually 47 days long.

People today sometimes choose to give up a special food they like, just as our ancestors gave up fat, butter and eggs. There are two main reasons for this: first, it is a symbol of discipline and commitment to God and, second, the money normally spent on the special food can be saved and given to a church or charity.

People can also choose to do something extra for Lent—perhaps studying the Bible and praying more, attending a Lent group or visiting a residential home and reading to some of the residents.

At the beginning of your pancake party, you could cut out a giant paper pancake and ask people to write their Lenten fast or resolution on it. Pray together for help to encourage everyone to carry out their intentions.

Pancake recipe

You will need:
- 100 g plain flour
- Pinch of salt
- 1 egg (beaten)
- 250 ml milk (or milk and water)
- 50 g fat

Mix the flour and salt in a basin, make a hollow in the centre and drop in the beaten egg. Stir with a wooden spoon and add milk gradually until all the flour is worked in. Beat well and add any remaining liquid.

For each pancake, melt a small amount of fat in a frying pan. When it begins to smoke, stir the batter and add 2 tablespoons to the pan. When golden underneath, turn or flip and cook on the other side. Add your own choice of filling.

Traditionally, pancakes are served with sugar and a squeeze of lemon juice.

Fantastic fillings

Different people from around the world have, of course, different ideas about what tastes good in pancakes. Why not try some of these:

- chocolate: Belgium
- lemon and sugar: Britain
- banana and coconut: Caribbean
- stir fry and prawns: China
- Brie, Camembert and French onion: France
- frankfurter and sauerkraut: Germany
- tomato and Mozzarella: Italy
- vegetable curry: India
- Emmenthal cheese and ham: Switzerland

International quiz

Here is a quiz to do in groups. Introduce the quiz by explaining that many countries have pancakes of one kind or another, although the pancakes have different names. Write on a flipchart all the names you can think of together. Then compare with the list below.

- Hot cakes (American)
- Pikelets (Australian)
- Nockerin (Austrian)
- Pancakes (British)
- Egg rolls (Chinese)
- Crêpes (French)
- Pfannkuchen (German)
- Palacsinta (Hungarian)
- Cannelloni (Italian)
- Blintzes (Jewish)
- Tortillas (Mexican)
- Lefser (Norwegian)
- Blini (Russian)
- Plattar (Swedish)
- Crempog (Welsh)

Then hand out copies of the wordsearch and find all those words in it. You could make this into a race.

Creative ideas for the preparation for Lent

```
C  A  N  N  E  L  L  O  N  I  E  F  A  S  X
O  T  H  Q  W  M  L  I  E  H  H  Q  E  L  N
S  D  O  C  X  E  W  S  H  Z  O  C  W  L  S
L  E  F  R  F  C  O  K  C  Z  T  R  Z  O  C
C  D  K  S  T  Z  V  L  U  Y  C  E  O  R  N
N  R  E  A  I  I  L  T  K  D  A  P  S  G  U
J  R  E  S  C  J  L  S  N  T  K  E  D  G  T
Q  P  V  M  X  N  E  L  N  U  E  S  P  E  F
R  K  L  H  P  Z  A  I  A  X  S  I  R  Y  Z
F  R  J  X  T  O  S  P  F  S  K  G  P  K  C
D  Y  K  N  J  C  G  R  P  E  I  N  I  L  B
S  I  I  E  A  V  W  P  L  A  T  T  A  R  G
P  L  K  L  W  I  I  E  K  O  R  O  I  D  B
B  C  A  U  O  I  T  N  I  R  E  K  C  O  N
U  P  L  Y  U  S  C  U  H  V  B  U  P  Z  M
```

BLINI	BLINTZES	CANNELLONI
CREMPOG	CREPES	EGGROLLS
HOTCAKES	LEFSER	NOCKERIN
PALACSINTA	PANCAKES	PFANNKUCHEN
PIKELETS	PLATTAR	TORTILLAS

Pancake quiz

In teams, see if you can come up with answers to the following questions:

1. How big was the world's biggest pancake?
   a) 5 metres   b) 10 metres   c) 15 metres

2. Shrove Tuesday marks the beginning of which church season?
   a) Christmas   b) Lent   c) Harvest

3. Which of these is the name given to Shrove Tuesday in some countries?
   a) Mardi Gras   b) St Nicholas Day   c) Noel

4. Which town in England has a famous pancake race every year?
   a) Portsmouth   b) Olney   c) Colchester

5. What's the prize for the winner?
   a) A new frying pan   b) A medal
   c) A kiss from the pancake bell ringer

6. What does 'Shrove' mean?
   a) Eating a lot   b) Confessing and being forgiven of your sins
   c) Getting slimmer

7. Which ingredient would you not find in a pancake?
   a) Flour   b) Baking powder   c) Eggs

Answers: 1c, 2b, 3a, 4b, 5c, 6b, 7b

The great egg challenge

For each team you will need:
A newspaper (make sure it's a suitable one for children to see); sticky tape; eight drinking straws; a piece of A4 card; scissors; string; two balloons

Each team has 20 minutes, using the materials provided, to create a way to transport a raw egg from a table to the floor without breaking it. When everyone has made their creation, get together, hand out the eggs and watch each team attempt the challenge. Award prizes for those who successfully transport their egg intact and for the most ingenious idea.

Tip: cover the floor with plastic to minimise the mess.

Pancake bingo

You will need:
- A selection of nine copyright-free images related to Pancake Day: use the pictures on page 20 or download some from the internet
- Cards divided into six squares, to make a different gameboard for each team
- Six blank squares of paper, the same size as the pictures, for each team
- A master pictureboard with all nine pictures on it
- Another complete set of nine pictures

In advance, make several photocopies of the nine pictures. Make gameboards for the teams by sticking six different pictures on to a piece of card. Every board must be different.

Give each team a board and six blank squares of paper to cover each picture as it is called.

Put your complete set of picture cards into a bag or box and pull them out one at a time. Call out the pictures in turn, covering each one on your master pictureboard as you go. When one team has a full board of pictures, they shout 'Pancake!'

You could play the game several times and keep score of who wins each time.

Pancake games

Cover a frisbee in brown paper so that it looks like a pancake, or just call your frisbee a pancake. Everyone stands around in a circle and is given the name of a country. One chosen person is the frying pan, who says, 'I send my pancake to...', names the person and their country and throws the pancake to them.

When the pancake is caught, that person has to name another country and throw it on.

Alternatively, why not try using the different names of the pancakes from the wordsearch?

Pancake races

Provide a selection of frying pans and make pretend pancakes using either carpet underlay, carpet squares or corrugated cardboard from supermarket boxes. Cut whichever material you use into circles (with cardboard you might need several layers stuck together to create enough weight).

Line up contestants at a starting line, each with a frying pan and pancake. On 'Go', they head towards the finishing line but they must flip the pancake ten times before reaching the line. Each contestant will need someone to count for them and stop any cheating.

✛

Creative ideas for the countdown to Easter

Many years ago, calendars were made to mark the passing of Lent (rather like Advent calendars). It's a useful way of counting the days between Ash Wednesday and Easter Day and will also help to show children that the time between Ash Wednesday to Easter Day is, in fact, more than 40 days.

French nun calendar

In France, Lenten calendars are still made in the shape of a nun. The nun has seven feet, one for each week in Lent. The calendar can be hung by a thread or attached to a wall and, at the end of each week, one of the nun's feet is tucked under until she is legless. The nun doesn't have a mouth because she appears to be fasting.

Greek kukuras

The Greek Lenten calendar is called a *kukuras* and is made from a large well-scrubbed potato and feathers.

You will need:
A large potato, well scrubbed; a length of string or strong yarn; seven large feathers

Make a hole right through the centre of the potato using a skewer or knitting needle. Thread a length of string or strong yarn through the hole and knot it firmly underneath the potato, so that the potato can be hung up. Either stick seven large feathers into the potato and pull one out for each week during Lent, or stick a feather into the potato each week during Lent.

Lenten chain calendar

You will need:
39 strips of purple paper; six strips of white paper; one strip of black paper; one strip of gold paper; stapler

Each strip of paper should be about 20 cm by 3 cm. The purple strips are for each weekday in Lent, the white strips are for each Sunday (if you like, you could use pink for Mothering Sunday and green for Palm Sunday), the black strip is for Good Friday and the gold strip is for Easter Sunday.

This calendar can be used in two ways. On Ash Wednesday, write a prayer on the first purple strip and staple it to make a circle. This will be the first link of the chain. On the next day, the first Thursday of Lent, write a prayer on the second strip, loop it through the first circle and staple it. Repeat this process for the first Friday and Saturday. On the first Sunday in Lent, write a prayer on a white strip of paper and attach it to the chain. Continue in this way until all the strips have been used, remembering to use the correct colours. It can be hung as a decoration for Easter.

Alternatively, start by making a chain of all the strips. Staple the first purple strip into a circle, then loop the second purple strip through the first circle and staple it. Add another two purple strips and then a white strip. Continue with all the strips until a long chain has been formed, getting the colours in the right place. Don't forget that Lent begins on Ash Wednesday, so the first week only has four purple strips. Hang the chain in a special place and remove one link for each day of Lent.

This is an easy way of showing children that Lent has more than 40 days.

Easter tree calendar

For this activity you will need eggs that can be hung on a branch. They could be decorations bought from a gift shop or you could make your own from cardboard and thread, which the children can decorate.

If you use a flowering branch or large twigs from the garden, they may well bloom in time for Easter. Alternatively, you could use an artificial tree.

You will need:
A branch or large twigs from a tree, securely placed in a pot;
47 eggs; large bowl or basket

Place the tree in position and put the eggs in the bowl or basket. Starting on Ash Wednesday, hang one egg on the tree every day during Lent. You might like to save a special egg for Easter Day.

You might like to have a supply of chocolate eggs (preferably wrapped) so that, every time an egg is hung on the tree, you can replace it in the bowl or basket with a chocolate egg. Try to wait until Easter Day to eat them.

To make your own eggs, you will need:
Thin card; scissors; hole punch; colouring pens or paints; thread for hanging

Draw an egg shape, copy it on to thin card and cut out 47 eggs. Decorate the eggs and make a small hole in the top of each card. Push a piece of thread through each hole and tie into a knot so that it will hang. You might like to put a date on each egg so that there's no confusion over which one to use.

✣

Creative ideas for Lent and Easter cooking

Simnel cake

A Simnel cake is a fruit cake with a layer of marzipan and eleven marzipan balls on the top, symbolising eleven of Jesus' disciples. The missing twelfth ball represents Judas Iscariot, who betrayed Jesus.

If you're making the cake for Mothering Sunday, you could decorate the top with sugar flowers instead of marzipan balls.

You will need:
- 110 g butter or margarine
- 110 g brown sugar
- 2 eggs
- 300 g self-raising flour
- ½ teaspoon mixed spice
- 350 g mixed dried fruit
- 2 tablespoons golden syrup
- 100 ml (approx.) milk to mix
- 700 g marzipan
- A little apricot jam
- 8-inch (20-cm) cake tin, greased and lined

Set the oven to 150°C (325°F, Gas 3).

Mix together the butter and sugar until they are creamy and then gently beat in the eggs. You may want to add a little flour with the eggs. Mix in the rest of the flour and mixed spice, then stir in the dried fruit and golden syrup. Add enough milk to make a dropping consistency.

Roll out about a third of the marzipan to make a circle the size of the cake tin. Place half the cake mixture in the tin, put the marzipan on top of the mixture, and place the remaining mixture on top. Smooth down the top.

Bake in the centre of the oven for 1 to 1¼ hours or until a thin metal skewer inserted in the centre of the cake comes out without a trace of stickiness.

Let the cake cool for about ten minutes and loosen the cake from the tin gently with a knife. Turn out on to a wire tray and allow to cool thoroughly.

Roll out another third of the marzipan to make a circle the size of the cake. Spread the apricot jam on the top of the cake and place the marzipan circle over the jam.

With the last third of the marzipan, make eleven equal-sized balls and arrange them around the outside of the cake. You may like to pop the cake under the grill for a few seconds to make it look golden.

If you haven't got time to bake a fruit cake, buy a fruit cake and decorate it on top with marzipan.

Hot cross buns

Hot cross buns are traditionally eaten on Good Friday, but these special buns pre-date the Christian festival. In earlier times, the bun represented the moon and the cross dividing it represented the four quarters of the moon.

In Britain, the Anglo-Saxons made small cakes marked with a cross to eat at their spring festival. Hot cross buns were banned by Oliver Cromwell but were brought back again with the restoration of the monarchy.

There are lots of superstitions surrounding hot cross buns. It was once believed that buns baked early on Good Friday would have special powers. If they were overcooked and allowed to harden, they could be kept for a year without going mouldy. These buns would then be used to try to cure common illnesses like dysentery and whooping cough.

Sailors thought that if they took a hot cross bun to sea with them, it would safeguard them from shipwreck and they would return home safely.

It is thought that the rhyme 'Hot cross buns' is an advertising cry from the time when bakers sold their wares in the street.

You will need:
- 1 kg plain flour
- 1 teaspoon salt
- 2 teaspoons mixed spice
- 125 g butter or margarine
- 125 g caster sugar
- 250 g currants
- Two 7g packets instant yeast
- 550 ml warm milk
- 2 eggs
- A little extra milk and sugar for glazing

These quantities will make about 24 buns.

Mix together the flour, salt and spices in a large mixing bowl. Cut the butter or margarine into small pieces, then rub it into the flour with fingertips until the mixture is like fine crumbs. Mix in the sugar and the currants.

Stir the yeast and milk together in another bowl and beat the eggs into the yeast liquid. Make a well in the middle of the dry ingredients and pour the yeast liquid into it. Mix well until a soft dough is formed. Cover with a clean cloth and leave to rise in a warm place for half an hour.

Grease some baking trays. Divide up the mixture and shape it into buns. Put the buns on the baking trays about 8 cm apart.

Leave the buns to rise again for about another 30 minutes. After about 20 minutes, set the oven to 220°C (425°F, Gas 7).

Cut a cross in the top of each bun with the back of a knife. Put the buns in the oven and bake for about 15–20 minutes.

When cooked, brush the buns with the milk and sugar and return them to the oven for a couple of minutes to dry.

Resurrection rolls

These rolls symbolise the resurrection of Jesus.

* The croissant represents the cloth in which Jesus was wrapped.
* The marshmallow represents Jesus.
* The melted butter represents the embalming oil.
* The cinnamon and sugar represent the anointing spices.
* Wrapping the marshmallow up inside the croissant represents the wrapping of Jesus' body after he had died.
* The oven represents the tomb. Opening the cooled croissant reminds us of the disciples opening the tomb and discovering that Jesus was no longer there. The marshmallow melts and the dough is puffed up but, like the tomb, it is empty.

You will need:
* 1 packet of croissant rolls, ready to cook (you can find this uncooked dough in the chiller section of most supermarkets)
* Large marshmallows
* 50 g butter, melted
* 1 tbsp cinnamon
* 1 tbsp sugar

Preheat the oven to 175°C (350°F, Gas 4).

Take a croissant dough triangle and a marshmallow. Dip the marshmallow into the melted butter and then into the cinnamon and the sugar.

Fold the dough into a croissant shape, wrapping the coated marshmallow tightly in the middle, ensuring that the marshmallow is sealed inside. Place croissants on a lightly greased baking tray and cook for 10–12 minutes.

When the croissants have cooled, they can be opened.

Easter story biscuits

Ideally, these biscuits are made the night before Easter. Tell the Easter story as you make them, using the outline below.

You will need:
- 150 g whole pecan nuts
- 1 teaspoon vinegar
- 3 egg whites
- Pinch of salt
- 200 g sugar
- Bible

Preheat the oven to 150°C (300°F, Gas 3).

Put the pecan nuts in the plastic bag and beat them with the wooden spoon to break them into small pieces. (Children will love doing this!) Explain that after Jesus was arrested, he was beaten by the Roman soldiers.

Read John 19:1–3:

Pilate gave orders for Jesus to be beaten with a whip. The soldiers made a crown out of thorn branches and put it on Jesus. Then they put a purple robe on him. They came up to him and said, 'Hey, you king of the Jews!' They also hit him with their fists.

Let the children smell the vinegar. Put one teaspoon of vinegar into a mixing bowl. Explain that when Jesus was thirsty on the cross, he was given cheap wine to drink, which would have tasted just like vinegar.

Read John 19:28–30:

Jesus knew that he had now finished his work. And in order to make the Scriptures come true, he said, 'I am thirsty!' A jar of cheap wine was there. Someone then soaked a sponge with the wine and held it up to Jesus' mouth on the stem of a hyssop plant. After Jesus drank the wine, he said, 'Everything is done!' He bowed his head and died.

Add egg whites to the vinegar. Egg represents life. Explain that Jesus gave his life to give us life.

Read John 10:10–11:

'I came so that everyone would have life, and have it fully. I am the good shepherd, and the good shepherd gives up his life for his sheep.'

Sprinkle a little salt into each child's hand. Let them taste it and brush the rest into the bowl. Explain that this represents the salty tears shed by Jesus' followers and the bitterness of the things we do wrong.

Read Luke 23:27:

A large crowd was following Jesus, and in the crowd a lot of women were crying and weeping for him.

So far, the ingredients are not very appetising. Add one cup of sugar. Explain that the sweetest part of the story is that Jesus died because he loved us. He wants us to know and belong to him.

Read Psalm 34:8 and John 3:16:

Discover for yourself that the Lord is kind. Come to him for protection, and you will be glad… God loved the people of this world so much that he gave his only Son, so that everyone who has faith in him will have eternal life and never really die.

Beat the ingredients together until stiff peaks are formed: you'll probably need to do this with an electric mixer. Explain that the colour white represents the purity in God's eyes of all those who have chosen to follow Jesus.

Read Isaiah 1:18 and John 3:1–3:

I, the Lord, invite you to come and talk it over. Your sins are scarlet red, but they will be whiter than snow or wool… There was a man named Nicodemus who was a Pharisee and a Jewish leader. One night he went to Jesus and said, 'Sir, we know that God has sent you to teach us. You could not perform these miracles unless God were with you.' Jesus replied, 'I tell you for certain that you must be born from above before you can see God's kingdom!'

Fold the broken pecan nuts into the mixture. Drop a spoonful of mixture on to the baking tray and repeat until all the mixture has been used up. Explain that each mound represents the rocky tomb where Jesus' body was laid.

Read Matthew 27:57–60:

That evening a rich disciple named Joseph from the town of Arimathea went and asked for Jesus' body. Pilate gave orders for it to be given to Joseph, who took the body and wrapped it in a clean linen cloth. Then Joseph put the body in his own tomb that had been cut into solid rock and had never been used. He rolled a big stone against the entrance to the tomb and went away.

Put the biscuits in the oven, close the door and turn the oven off. Give each child a piece of sticky tape and ask them to seal the oven door. Explain that Jesus' tomb was sealed.

Read Matthew 27:65–66:

Pilate said to them, 'All right, take some of your soldiers and guard the tomb as well as you know how.' So they sealed it tight and placed soldiers there to guard it.'

Go to bed! Explain that the children may feel sad to leave the biscuits in the oven overnight. Jesus' followers were in despair when the tomb was sealed.

Read John 16:20:

'I tell you for certain that you will cry and be sad, but the world will be happy. You will be sad, but later you will be happy.'

On Easter morning, open the oven and give everyone a biscuit. Notice the cracked surface and take a bite: the biscuits are hollow. Explain that on the first Easter, Jesus' followers were amazed to find the tomb open and empty.

Read Matthew 28:1–9:

The Sabbath was over, and it was almost daybreak on Sunday when Mary Magdalene and the other Mary went to see the tomb. Suddenly a strong earthquake struck, and the Lord's angel came down from heaven. He rolled away the stone and sat on it. The angel looked as bright as lightning, and his clothes were white as snow. The guards shook from fear and fell down, as though they were dead.

The angel said to the women, 'Don't be afraid! I know you are looking for Jesus, who was nailed to a cross. He isn't here! God has raised him to life, just as Jesus said he would. Come, see the place where his body was lying. Now hurry! Tell his disciples that he has been raised to life and is on his way to Galilee. Go there, and you will see him. That is what I came to tell you.'

The women were frightened and yet very happy, as they hurried from the tomb and ran to tell his disciples. Suddenly Jesus met them and greeted them. They went near him, held on to his feet, and worshipped him.

Eggy bread for Easter

You will need:
A slice of bread; butter or similar spread; an egg

Heat the oven to 220°C (400°F, Gas 6). Lightly grease a baking sheet.

Spread the butter on to one side of the bread, then press a large biscuit cutter into the middle of the bread. Lift out the shape you have cut and put both pieces of bread on to a baking sheet, with the buttered sides upwards.

Break the egg on to a saucer. Then carefully slide the egg into the hole in the bread. Put the baking sheet in the oven. Bake the bread and egg for seven minutes, or a little longer if you don't like a runny egg yolk.

Wearing oven gloves, carefully lift the baking sheet out of the oven and lift the pieces of toast on to a plate. Eat immediately.

Chirpy chick cakes

You will need:
- 40 g butter, softened
- 75 g icing sugar
- 1 teaspoon lemon juice
- 1 drop of yellow food colouring
- 8 small fairy cakes, easily available in supermarkets
- Small round sweets and jelly diamonds

Put the butter into a bowl and beat it with a wooden spoon until it is creamy. Then stir in half of the icing sugar. Add the lemon juice and yellow food colouring and the rest of the icing sugar. Mix everything together well.

Using a blunt knife, cover the top of each cake with butter icing and use a fork to make the icing look feathery. Press two small round sweets on to each cake to make eyes. Cut the jelly diamonds in half and press the two halves into the icing on each cake to make a beak. Make the pointed ends of the halves stick up a little.

Flower sweets

You will need:
A little icing sugar; ready-to-roll icing; small jelly sweets

Sprinkle a little icing sugar on to a clean work surface and also on to a rolling pin. Roll out the icing until it is about 5 mm thick. Then use a small flower-shaped cutter to cut out shapes from the icing. Put a sweet on to the middle of each flower and press it down. Lift the flowers on to the baking sheet with a blunt knife.

Press the scraps into a ball, roll out the icing again and make more flowers. Leave them on a baking sheet for a couple of hours to harden.

Ascension cake

This is called Ascension cake because the fruit stays on the bottom of the cake, on the pastry, while the sponge 'rises' to heaven. The sugar sprinkled on the top represents the clouds that we see when looking up to the sky.

You will need:
- 200 g shortcrust pastry
- 4–6 tablespoons jam or mincemeat
- 125 g glacé cherries, chopped
- 50 g sultanas
- 50 g flaked almonds
- 185 g sponge mix and the ingredients to make it up
- 1 tablespoon ground almonds

Preheat the oven to 190°C (375°F, Gas 5). Grease and line an 18 cm square tin.

Roll out the pastry to a rectangle, slightly larger than the tin, and ease it into the bottom of the tin. Prick the base with a fork and chill for 15 minutes.

Spread the pastry base with jam or mincemeat and cover with cherries, sultanas and flaked almonds.

Make up the sponge mix as directed and add the ground almonds. Spoon the mixture into the tin and bake for 35–40 minutes, until golden and just firm.

Cut the cake into squares and serve warm or cold, sprinkled with sugar.

Tiramisu

Tiramisu translates from Italian as 'Lift me up', so it would make a wonderful treat for Ascension Day.

You will need:
- 568 ml double cream
- 250 g mascarpone
- 75 ml marsala wine (if you are making tiramisu for adults only)

- 5 tablespoons golden caster sugar
- 300 ml strong coffee (made with 2 tablespoons coffee granules and 300 ml boiling water)
- 175 g sponge fingers
- 25 g dark chocolate
- 2 teaspoons cocoa powder

Put the cream, marscarpone, marsala (if you are using it) and sugar in a large bowl. Whisk until the cream and marscarpone have completely combined and have the consistency of thickly whipped cream.

Put the coffee into a medium-sized shallow dish and dip in a few sponge fingers at a time, turning for a few seconds until they are nicely soaked but not soggy. Layer the sponge into a serving dish until you have used half the sponge fingers, then spread over half of the creamy mixture.

Grate most of the chocolate over the cream and repeat the layers, finishing with the creamy mixture. Cover and chill for a few hours or overnight.

To serve, dust with cocoa powder and grate over the remainder of the chocolate.

Heavenly jellies

You will need:
Blue jelly; whipping or double cream

Make up the jelly according to the instructions and allow to cool. Whip the cream until it is very stiff.

When the jelly is almost set, spoon it into serving glasses and layer with whipped cream to make 'clouds'. Leave to set in the fridge.

Creative ideas for Lent and Easter prayers

Sacred space for prayer

Think about creating time in the day for praying together as a family. You might want to make a promise to each other that you will try to do this every day during Lent.

Make a 'sacred space' to encourage quiet reflection and prayer in your home during Lent. This space could be:

- A corner of a room
- A shelf
- A corner of a shed or garage
- A table in your hall, if you have one

Equip your sacred space with a piece of cloth, a cross, a candle, a Bible, a picture of Jesus, or some natural objects such as pebbles, shells and feathers. The traditional colour used in churches in Lent is purple, so you could use a purple cloth. (The colour changes to red on Palm Sunday.)

Another way of praying together is to use the 'examen', which is a Christian practice that involves reflecting on the day and thinking about when you felt close to God and when you felt far from God. You might like to end your reflection by saying the Lord's Prayer together or by saying a simple prayer like the one below.

Father God, thank you for today.
We are grateful for the good things... (everyone could say one thing out loud).

We bring before you the hard things… (say something, if appropriate).
Help us to remember that you are always with us. Amen

Candle prayers for Lent

This series of prayers is more suitable for use in church, at the beginning of a service, than at home. The liturgy is based on the ancient Good Friday service of Tenebrae, which makes use of gradually diminishing light.

You will need a display of six purple candles and one large, distinctive white one. If you plan to use the alternative prayers for the Fourth Sunday of Lent, use one pink candle instead of a purple one. This is for Mothering Sunday, a day of celebration in the middle of Lent.

On the first Sunday of Lent, light all the candles before the service. As you say the prayer for each Sunday, extinguish one of the candles. On subsequent Sundays, light all except those that have already been ceremonially extinguished. The Christ candle, only extinguished on Good Friday, needs to be at the front, as it will burn lowest. Keep this one candle and relight it on Easter Day.

The First Sunday of Lent

We have these Lenten candles to remind us of Christ, the light of the world, whose light was taken from the world on the cross.

We extinguish this candle, O Lord. For whenever we sin, whenever we turn from your paths, we extinguish a small part of your light in our world. Help us to fight against sin, the world and the devil.

Lord in your mercy,
Hear our prayer.

The Second Sunday of Lent

We have these Lenten candles to remind us of Christ, the light of the world, whose light was taken from the world on the cross.

We extinguish this candle, O Lord. For whenever we do wrong, whenever we ignore Christ, whenever we turn from your teaching, we spoil and lessen the presence of Christ's light in the world. Help us to further Christ's kingdom here on earth, to show us the way to God's eternal kingdom in heaven.

Lord in your mercy,
Hear our prayer.

The Third Sunday of Lent

We have these Lenten candles to remind us of Christ, the light of the world, whose light was taken from the world on the cross.

We extinguish this candle, O Lord. For whenever there is suffering, whenever your image is marred by human cruelty and thoughtlessness, the light that you are in the world is dimmed. Help us to fight against suffering and to keep your light shining in your creation.

Lord in your mercy,
Hear our prayer.

The Fourth Sunday of Lent

We have these Lenten candles to remind us of Christ, the light of the world, whose light was taken from the world on the cross.

We extinguish this candle, O Lord, as a token that although you shone at the transfiguration as a light of hope to the disciples, that light of hope was later extinguished for them. Help us, with the light of faith, to transfigure our lives, that we may always hope and trust in you.

Lord in your mercy,
Hear our prayer.

Alternative prayer for Mothering Sunday

We have these Lenten candles to remind us of Christ, the light of the world, whose light was taken from the world on the cross.

We extinguish this candle, O Lord. Jesus, born of the Blessed Mary, you came as a light to all your children who believe and trust in you. Your life, that light, was extinguished on the cross of Good Friday. But may we, your children, always keep within us the light of the hope of faith.

Lord in your mercy,
Hear our prayer.

The Fifth Sunday of Lent (Passion Sunday)

We have these Lenten candles to remind us of Christ, the light of the world, whose light was taken from the world on the cross.

We extinguish this candle, O Lord. It symbolises how your Son, the light of the world whom we follow in faith, was put to death on the cross for our salvation. May the cross and passion of our Lord be a light to us in the world, no matter how dark our paths may be.

Lord in your mercy,
Hear our prayer.

The Sixth Sunday of Lent (Palm Sunday)

We have these Lenten candles to remind us of Christ, the light of the world, whose light was taken from the world on the cross.

We extinguish this candle, O Lord, to remind ourselves that the false praises and cheers of the crowds in the light of day turned to the darkness of Gethsemane and Golgotha. May we follow your light and shun the false light given by the praise of the world.

Lord in your mercy,
Hear our prayer.

Good Friday

We have these Lenten candles to remind us of Christ, the light of the world, whose light was taken from the world on the cross.

We extinguish this candle, O Lord. At the sixth hour there was darkness over the whole land until the ninth hour. At this moment your life, the light of the world, departed from your creation. From this darkness, may new light come.

Lord in your mercy,
Hear our prayer.

On Easter Sunday, the large white candle can be relit.

Mothering Sunday prayer

You will need a selection of props, as listed below.

Say that mums play many different and important roles in family life. Pull out your props one at a time and talk about some of the tasks that mums carry out. For example:

- Whisk: they cook for us.
- Bandage: they look after us when we're injured.
- Medicine: they nurse us when we're ill.
- Car keys: they take us to places (to school, to church, to see our friends).
- Washing powder: they wash and iron our clothes.
- Screwdriver: they mend things.
- Storybook: they tell us stories.
- Exercise book: they help us with homework.
- A big paper heart: they go on and on loving us, even when we're naughty.

Give out the props to a number of different people and ask them each to say a one-line prayer, thanking God that mums do those particular things for us. Alternatively, say a concluding 'thank you' prayer yourself, weaving in all the different roles mentioned.

Instead of mothers, you could talk about other people who care for us. You can also adapt this activity for use on Fathers' Day, remembering that we enjoy the privilege of having two fathers, one on earth and one in heaven.

Palm leaf prayers

You will need:
Green paper cut into palm leaf shapes, one for each child (see template on page 128); pens; brown paper cut into the shape of a tree trunk; backing paper; glue

Read the words of praise that the crowd shouted as Jesus rode into Jerusalem, in John 12:12–13.

Encourage everyone to write their own one-line praise prayers on the palm leaves (for example, 'Jesus, you're amazing!' or 'Jesus, you're the best friend ever!').

Mount the palm tree trunk on to backing paper and paste the palm leaf prayers around the top to make a prayer collage.

If you have a large cardboard tube (a carpet tube would be ideal) this could be used as a tree trunk. Paint the tube brown or wrap brown paper securely around it, and stick the palm leaf prayers on to it at the top.

Hot cross bun prayers

You will need:
Enough hot cross buns for everyone to try; butter (optional); plate

Hold up a hot cross bun and ask the group if they know why we eat these buns on Good Friday. Say that millions of people in different countries eat hot cross buns to remember how Jesus suffered on the cross for our wrongdoing.

Think about some of the ingredients needed to make the buns. Yeast is needed to make the buns rise; it can also remind us that Jesus did not stay dead but rose again. Dried fruits are added to the mixture; these remind us of the good things that come from Jesus' death. Without his death on the cross, we would not be able to enjoy new life.

Pass around the hot cross buns and, in a time of quiet, invite everyone to take a piece and eat it. As the group does this, encourage everyone to take this opportunity to thank Jesus silently in their heart for his willingness to die so that we might live.

Triumph of light prayer

You will need:
A relighting candle (test it first); a box of matches

Light the candle and talk about how we might think of Jesus' death as the darkness trying to put out the light. Blow the candle out. As it relights, say that Jesus' power was greater than the darkness and he came back to life.

Say the following prayer, with everyone joining in the responses.

Thank you, Jesus, for your love for us.
Hallelujah! Jesus is the King!
Thank you for suffering so that we can have new life.
Hallelujah! Jesus is the King!
We praise you because you defeated death.
Hallelujah! Jesus is the King!
Help us to know you are close to us always.
Hallelujah! Jesus is the King!
Amen

Floral cross prayer

You will need:
A large piece of brown card; flower shapes cut from brightly
coloured paper; pens; glue

In advance, cut out a large cross from the card (if possible, use corrugated card to give a textured effect). Talk about how the cross reminds us of the events of Good Friday. In fact, Good Friday is not a 'good' day at all, but a very sad day on which we remember that Jesus was put to death on the cross even though he had done nothing wrong. Some people think that the name Good Friday may have derived from 'God's Friday', just as 'goodbye' comes from the phrase 'God be with you'. Others believe that we call the day Good Friday because, in the old days, the word 'good' was often used to mean 'holy'. In many European languages, Good Friday is called 'Great Friday'. On Good Friday Jesus certainly did a very great thing for all humankind. He gave his life for our wrongdoing, so that all who believe in him might be free.

The cross is a symbol of Jesus' death, but Jesus did not stay on the cross: he rose again, and so it is also a symbol of our new life in him. Give out the flower shapes and invite everyone to write a short prayer on their flower, thanking Jesus for his amazing love. Young children could just draw a happy face.

Play some rousing Easter music and invite everyone to come up and stick their flower prayers on to the cross.

'The angel rolled the stone away' prayer

Make a 'tomb' with one hand by curling the fingers round, with the first finger and thumb in a circle shape, as the entrance to the tomb. The other hand, shaped as a fist, becomes the stone blocking the entrance. Each time the children say, 'The angel rolled the stone away', roll the fist away to reveal the empty tomb.

Thank you, Lord God, for Easter Day.
The angel rolled the stone away.

Thank you, Lord God, for raising Jesus from the dead.
The angel rolled the stone away.

Thank you, Lord God, for taking away our fear of death.
The angel rolled the stone away.

Thank you, Lord God, for loving us so much through Jesus.
The angel rolled the stone away.

Thank you, Lord God, for giving us hope and a new start.
The angel rolled the stone away.

Thank you, Lord God, for giving us a message of love to share with others.
The angel rolled the stone away.

Thank you, Lord God, for Easter Day.
The angel rolled the stone away.

Creative uses for Easter cards

Computer wallpaper

Scan your favourite cards into the computer and make them into a montage using a photo programme or Publisher programme. Use the montage as wallpaper or a screensaver at Easter. Children enjoy doing this and it can make a good memento of Easter if done every year.

Todder's lacing card

Make a lacing card for a toddler. Choose a suitable card, perhaps with a picture of an Easter egg on it, and laminate it. Punch holes around the edge using a hole punch and provide a brightly coloured shoelace to go in and out of the holes.

Easter confetti

Use a plain hole punch and an Easter-shaped hole punch (an egg or a chick, perhaps) and punch shapes from old Easter cards. This activity keeps children occupied for hours and the shapes can be popped into the envelopes of any Easter cards you send, to surprise the recipients.

Jigsaw eggs

Cut out egg shapes from the pictures on Easter cards. Cut each egg shape in half, zig-zag style, across the middle to resemble an egg breaking open. When you have prepared several eggs, hide them around the house (or your meeting space) and encourage the children to go and find two halves of a whole egg. Tell them that they can only carry one half of an egg at any time. Whoever collects the most eggs by getting lots of matching halves wins.

If you have two or three copies of the same card, make sure the zig-zag cut is different on each card: this will make it more difficult to find the matching pairs.

Easter greeting card puzzle

You will need:
An old Easter card; a piece of card, the same size as the Easter card; glue; scissors; felt-tip pens; pencil; ruler

Stick the picture on to the piece of card and write a greeting on the back.

Using the pencil, lightly draw the shapes you want to cut out to make a jigsaw puzzle. You might want squares or crazy shapes. Cut the card into pieces, carefully following the pencil lines. When you've done that, put the puzzle in an envelope and send it to a friend or relative.

Easter boxes

Make little Easter boxes that can be used as gift boxes on the Easter table, with a few small eggs or homemade sweets inside.

You will need:
Copies of the Easter box template, one per person (see page 129); Easter cards; scissors; glue; small gifts, wrapped Easter eggs or sweets

Copy the box template on to the back of a Easter card picture, or stick it on, and cut it out. (You may need to adjust the size to fit your chosen card.) Make up the box by glueing the tabs, and don't forget to pop a small gift inside before sticking the lid down.

Gift bags

Save good-quality brown or coloured paper bags, preferably without labels. Cut an attractive picture out of an Easter card and stick it to the front of the bag. Add a ribbon bow above the picture and wrap a gift in tissue paper before putting it in the bag. Brown paper bags with yellow and gold ribbon look very attractive.

Old birthday cards could also be used to make gift bags for birthday presents.

Easter bingo

You will need:
- A selection of Easter cards or wrapping paper, or nine copyright-free Easter images: use the pictures on page 50 or download some from the internet
- Cards divided into six squares, to make a different gamebaord for each team
- Six blank squares of paper, the same size as the pictures, for each team
- A master pictureboard with all nine pictures on it
- Another complete set of the nine pictures

In advance, make several photocopies of the nine pictures. Make gameboards for the teams by sticking six different pictures on to a piece of card. Every board must be different.

Give each team a board and six blank squares of paper to cover each picture as it is called.

Put your complete set of picture cards into a bag or box and pull them out one at a time. Call out the pictures in turn, covering each one on your master pictureboard as you go. If a team has that picture on their gameboard, they cover it with a counter or square of blank paper.

The first person to cover all their pictures shouts, 'Jesus is risen!' because these are the words people said when they discovered that Jesus was alive again.

Celebrating Lent at home

Christmas tree cross

How symbolic to use the trunk of your Christmas tree to count the days to Easter during Lent! It will need a bit of forward planning; if you haven't got a real Christmas tree, use some wood.

> **You will need:**
> A Christmas tree trunk; woodworking tools; glue and nails; six purple candles and one white candle

To make a Christmas tree cross, trim away the branches from the trunk and cut two pieces for the cross, one about 40 cm long and the other about 34 cm long. Make a notch in the longer piece, about one third from the end, and another in the middle of the shorter piece. Fit the pieces together snugly. You may want to use a couple of small nails to fasten the wood securely.

Drill seven holes for the candles to fit into, three below the crosspiece on the upright section of the cross, three across the crosspiece and one above the crosspiece. Put the white candle in the hole above the crosspiece and the purple candles in the other holes. You may like to decorate the cross with greenery.

On the first Sunday in Lent, light one of the purple candles during a family time together. On the second Sunday, light two purple candles. Continue in this way every Sunday during Lent, and on Easter Sunday light the white candle.

You may need to buy more than one set of candles, depending on how long you burn them.

Soap cross

The ash cross put on our foreheads at Ash Wednesday reminds us that we need to say 'sorry' for our wrongdoings and ask God to forgive us. A cross carved from soap is a reminder of how Jesus washed away our sins on the cross.

You will need:
A bar of soft hand soap; a knife; a pencil

Draw a cross shape on the bar of soap and carefully carve away the excess soap. If you save the soap chips, they can be put in a bottle with a little water added to make liquid soap.

As you wash with the soap cross, remember to thank God for forgiving us.

A Lent journal

What does Lent suggest to you? Deprivation? A time of giving things up? No chocolate? Why not make this year different and take up something for Lent as a family? Keep a journal, just for 47 days. Give up a little time each day to reflect on God's word and make a record of the things that strike you. Family members can take it in turns to put something in the journal, or everyone might like to add some musings to some pages.

> **You will need:**
> 47 pieces of A5 paper; one piece of thick A5 card; one piece of thin A5 card; hole punch; ribbon or string; pens, decorations and so on

Stack the pieces of paper and card, with the thick card at the bottom and the thin card at the top. Arrange them in landscape orientation (with the shorter ends at the sides). Punch two holes in the left-hand side of the stack, making sure that the holes line up.

Decorate the thin card cover by drawing, painting or sticking on pictures. Thread ribbon or string through the holes and tie it firmly. Carefully score the card cover next to the holes so that it will open and the book can lie flat. Write the dates of Lent and Holy Week, one on each page.

Try to write in the journal every day during Lent. You could include something to do with a Bible study course you are following, or simply something on which to focus your thoughts.

If you've given something up for Lent, you could keep a note of how you're coping with the loss and how its absence has changed the way you respond to God.

Crown of thorns wreath

> **You will need:**
> A wreath that resembles a crown of thorns; six purple candles and one white candle; greenery; candle holders (optional)

You can buy ready-made wreaths from garden centres, but you could make your own from willow twigs or lengths of honeysuckle or vine.

Make your wreath by twining lengths of the branches together into a circle. Place six purple candles around the wreath and put one white candle in the centre. You could decorate the wreath with greenery.

To use this wreath, light one of the purple candles in the first week of Lent, two in the second week, and so on.

During Holy Week, you may like to light all six candles on Palm Sunday, five on Monday, four on Tuesday and so on, extinguishing one each day so that you end up with no candles lit on the Saturday before Easter Day. On Easter Sunday, light the white candle. You could light all the purple candles, too, on Easter Day.

Egg and spoon obstacle course

You will need:
Spoons; mini Easter eggs

When Jesus was in the desert, he was tempted by the devil to step off the right path. Jesus knew he needed to trust God and stay on the right path. Discuss with family members any times when they may have been tempted.

Set out an obstacle course in the house or garden. It could be made simply from furniture, cushions, boxes, hula hoops or anything else that you have to hand. Each person has to walk through the course as quickly as possible, carrying the egg on the spoon without letting it fall off.

To make the game a little harder, try putting the egg inside a cardboard tube and walking through the course without letting the egg roll out. (It's cheating to hold the end of the tube!)

Talk about how difficult it can be to stay on the right path sometimes. Perhaps a member of the family has tried to give up sweets for Lent and then been tempted during the first week and given in. How does it feel when you give in? How does it feel when you don't give in?

Pray together, asking God to help you stay on the right road when you face temptation.

Celebrating Ash Wednesday

Ash Wednesday is the first day of Lent, a time to ask for and receive forgiveness. Here are some activities you could do together to celebrate the day.

- Read Matthew 4:1–11 together. In this passage Jesus is tempted by the devil.
- Read Matthew 6:5–18 together. In this passage Jesus teaches about prayer and fasting.
- Make a desert tray. Cover the base of a tray or plastic box with a layer of sand. Add some stones and bare twigs or cacti. This arrangement could be adapted to become an Easter garden at the end of Lent.
- In some churches, on Ash Wednesday the previous year's palm crosses are burned. The ash is then used to make a cross on people's foreheads as a sign of forgiveness. At home, use ash mixed with a little water to make the sign of a cross on a window. As you do this, you could say the following prayer of St Richard of Chichester: 'Help us, Lord, to see you more clearly, love you more dearly and follow you more nearly, day by day. Amen'
- Do some spring cleaning: take old clothes (in good condition) to a charity shop; put away children's pictures that have been around for a while, to allow space for new ones.
- Traditionally, the game of marbles was played during Lent, beginning on Ash Wednesday. You could organise a family tournament.
- Say the Lord's Prayer together.

- Try to eat more simply, perhaps having one main meal per day and restricting other meals to light snacks. Make the main meal special. Choose a special grace to use throughout Lent. You might even try lentils in Lent!
- Wonder together about the story of Jesus being tempted in the desert.
  * Why was Jesus tempted?
  * Why did Jesus have these particular temptations?
  * What does this story say to us today?
  * What must we do about it?

Celebrating Mothering Sunday

Mothering Sunday is a brief escape from the discipline of Lent, to celebrate mothers. Also, drawing on old traditions, it is a celebration of the 'mother church'. Here are some activities you could do together at home.

- Read a Bible passage together. You could choose from the following:
  * Hannah's longing for a child and her joy at Samuel's birth (1 Samuel 1—2)
  * Jesus and his family visiting the temple (Luke 2:41–52)
  * God's mother-love for the people of Israel (Hosea 11:3–4)
  * God's mother-love for Jerusalem (Isaiah 66:7–13)
- Give mum breakfast in bed.
- Try to go to church as a family.
- Spend a few moments looking at the logo of the International Year of the Family (celebrating its 20th anniversary in 2014) on the internet. What do you see in it? What does it say to you about being a family? Make a logo or crest for your family.
- Make 'thank you' cards for the mothers and carers you know.

- Pick some spring flowers and make them into buttonholes to give to people.
- Make a thank-you tree. Place a tree branch securely in a plant pot and hang covered sweets from it. On luggage labels, write good things about each other and hang them on the branch, too. At the end of the day, share out the sweets.
- Make, or buy, a Simnel cake for tea time.
- Give each other a special hug.
- Wonder together about the following questions.
  - * Is your church really like a mother?
  - * Is your church really like a family?
  - * Why are families not always happy?
  - * How can families celebrate Mothering Sunday in a world of commercialism?

Resurrection eggs

Resurrection eggs are a different way of telling the story of Easter to young children. They are a set of twelve eggs that you open up, one a day, in the twelve days leading up to Easter. Each egg except the last contains an object and a verse that talks about a part of the Easter story.

Put the relevant item(s) and Bible verse in a plastic egg and write the number on the outside of the egg. Place them all in an egg box, which you can decorate if you like. Open one each day, starting on the Wednesday before Palm Sunday. This means that the last (empty) egg will be opened on Easter Day.

You will need:
Twelve plastic eggs that open; an egg carton for twelve eggs; paper and pens; felt-tip pen; the props for each day (as described below)

Here are some suggestions for the items inside the eggs.

1. A small leaf to represent a palm branch used at Jesus' triumphal entry into Jerusalem.
2. A small piece of bread and perhaps a thimble to represent the bread and wine at the Last Supper.
3. Some 5p pieces to represent the 30 pieces of silver that Judas Iscariot received.
4. A small piece of purple fabric or paper and a small piece of a thorny plant to represent the crown of thorns and purple robe.
5. A small piece of strong string with a knot tied in it to represent the soldiers whipping Jesus.
6. A tiny cross.
7. Three small nails.
8. A small piece of paper with the letters INRI written on it, to represent the sign nailed on to the cross ('Jesus of Nazareth, King of the Jews').
9. A tiny piece of sponge and a cocktail stick with the end broken off to represent the sponge used to give Jesus a drink and the spear that pierced his side.
10. A small amount of mixed spice (or other spice) wrapped in a small piece of fabric or paper to represent the burial traditions.
11. A small stone or pebble to represent the stone rolled in front of, and away from the tomb.
12. The last egg is empty, to represent the empty tomb.

1: Palm branch

To recognise how Jesus was celebrated when he entered Jerusalem.

> Many people spread clothes on the road, while others put
> down branches which they had cut from trees. Some people
> walked ahead of Jesus and others followed behind. They were
> all shouting, 'Hooray for the Son of David! God bless the one
> who comes in the name of the Lord. Hooray for God in heaven
> above!'
>
> MATTHEW 21:8–9

2: Bread

To signify the Last Supper.

> During the meal Jesus took some bread in his hands. He
> blessed the bread and broke it. Then he gave it to his disciples
> and said, 'Take this and eat it. This is my body.'
>
> MATTHEW 26:26

3: Silver coins

To show the bribe that Jesus took to betray Jesus.

> Judas had betrayed Jesus, but when he learnt that Jesus had
> been sentenced to death, he was sorry for what he had done.
> He returned the thirty silver coins to the chief priests and
> leaders.
>
> MATTHEW 27:3

4: Purple cloth and thorns

To acknowledge the soldiers mocking Jesus.

> Pilate wanted to please the crowd. So he set Barabbas free.
> Then he ordered his soldiers to beat Jesus with a whip and nail
> him to a cross.
>
> MARK 15:15

5: Rope (whip)

To signify the beating that Jesus had to endure.

> They stripped off Jesus' clothes and put a scarlet robe on him.
> They made a crown out of thorn branches and placed it on his
> head, and they put a stick in his right hand. The soldiers knelt
> down and pretended to worship him. They made fun of him and
> shouted, 'Hey, you king of the Jews!'
>
> MATTHEW 27:28–29

6: Cross

To show the physical burden that Jesus had to carry.

> Jesus carried his cross to a place known as 'The Skull'. In
> Aramaic this place is called 'Golgotha'.
>
> JOHN 19:17

7: Nails

To show the pain that Jesus went through when he was crucified.

> They nailed Jesus to a cross and gambled to see who would get his clothes.
>
> MARK 15:24

8: INRI sign

To recognise Pilate's admission that Jesus was indeed the long-awaited king.

> On the cross was a sign that told why he was nailed there. It read, 'This is the King of the Jews.'
>
> MARK 15:26

9: Sponge and spear

To signify the last moments of Jesus' life and proof of his death.

> A jar of cheap wine was there. Someone then soaked a sponge with the wine and held it up to Jesus' mouth on the stem of a hyssop plant... But when they came to Jesus, they saw that he was already dead, and they did not break his legs. One of the soldiers stuck his spear into Jesus' side, and blood and water came out.
>
> JOHN 19:29, 33–34

10: Spices

To represent the burial procedures.

> The two men wrapped the body in a linen cloth, together with the spices, which was how the Jewish people buried their dead.
>
> JOHN 19:40

11: Stone

To show that the tomb has been opened.

> On Sunday morning while it was still dark, Mary Magdalene went to the tomb and saw that the stone had been rolled away from the entrance.
>
> JOHN 20:1

12: Nothing

To show that Jesus has risen.

> 'Jesus isn't here! He has been raised from death. Remember that while he was still in Galilee, he told you, "The Son of Man will be handed over to sinners who will nail him to a cross. But three days later he will rise to life."'
>
> LUKE 24:6–7

Reproduced with permission from *Creative Ideas for Lent and Easter* by Jane Tibbs (Barnabas for Children, 2014) www.barnabasinchurches.org.uk

Creative ideas with the number 40

Lent is 40 days long, not counting the Sundays. Here is a selection of activities to be used as a reminder. Some are very suitable for younger children, others for older children.

Necklace with 40 beads

You will need:
A piece of string or yarn cut to the desired length for a necklace for each child; pots containing macaroni pasta, sprayed gold, silver and other colours; a tub for each child; Sellotape

Give each child a piece of string with a large knot tied in one end. Encourage children to count 40 assorted pieces of macaroni into their tub. Thread pasta on to the string; it's helpful to put a piece of Sellotape on the end of the string to make a kind of needle. Tie ends firmly together.

40 hunt

You will need:
Forty number '40's on pieces of paper; sticky tack; pens and paper

Before children arrive, hide the 40 pieces of paper around the room in fairly unusual places. When children arrive, tell them you have hidden lots of number 40s around the room. In pairs, the children hunt for the 40s and write down where they have seen them. Award a small prize for the pairs who count the right number of 40s.

It might be a good idea to write the numbers 1 to 40 down the side of a sheet of paper for the children to write alongside.

40 letters

Think of 40 people who have touched your life in some way. Every day, write a letter to one of them and pray for them.

40-day resolutions

Here are some suggestions for some Lenten resolutions:

- Collect 40 tins of soup (or something similar) to be given to a centre for the homeless or a day care centre or sent to refugees.
- Collect 40 toys in good condition for a local children's day centre, play group or after-school club.
- Collect 40 story books for a doctor's or dentist's waiting room. (You will need to check first for a suitable recipient.)
- Raise money to buy 40 Bibles for your church (if they are needed) or a church abroad.
- If everyone collected 40 pennies (or 2p pieces or 20p pieces) how much would you raise all together?

Celebrating Holy Week at home

Preparing for Holy Week

Here are some simple ways of celebrating the events of Holy Week that will require a small amount of advance preparation.

Green hill

Spread damp cotton wool over an upturned bowl and sprinkle cress seeds on it. They will grow into a 'green hill' in time for Good Friday and will be ready to eat in egg sandwiches on Easter Day. The hill is mentioned in the first verse of the traditional hymn 'There is a green hill far away, without a city wall'.

Collect some pussy willow and catkins to decorate the house.

Easter garden

You will need:
A shallow dish or tray; soil or potting compost; moss, grass or sand; twigs and thread; small pot; a stone; egg cups; small flowers; gravel

Place the soil or potting compost in the tray and arrange it to make a hill to one side. Cover the soil with moss, grass or sand. Make three crosses from the twigs and press them into the 'hillside'. Put the small pot into the hillside to make a tomb and place the stone close to the mouth of the tomb. Place egg cups full of flowers in the soil around the garden. Use the gravel to make a path coming from the tomb.

On Good Friday or Holy Saturday, cover the entrance to the tomb with the stone. On Easter morning, move the stone away from the tomb, showing that it is empty.

Palm Sunday

On Palm Sunday we remember Jesus coming in triumph to Jerusalem, the religious and political capital of Israel. He is greeted as a king but he rides on a donkey. The crowds are full of happiness but Jesus cries over the city. The crowds live for today but Jesus is only too aware of the danger in store.

Read Luke 19:28–38 together, which is the story of Jesus' entry into Jerusalem.

Play 'stick the tail on the donkey' to remember that donkeys are often seen as figures of fun.

Wonder together about the following questions:

- Why did Jesus have to be so humble?
- How can people be so fickle and unreliable?
- Why was Jesus sad when he looked at Jerusalem?

Jesus dying and rising

The four days when we commemorate the passion, death and resurrection of Jesus are a time for:

- Remembering and praying
- Remembering and asking for forgiveness
- Remembering and waiting
- Rejoicing, dancing and singing

In these four days the story moves quickly and, for the disciples, the mood changes dramatically. On Maundy Thursday, Jesus shared the Passover with them. For him, there was foreboding; for them, it was like any other special meal, enjoyed in the present.

Prepare together by using the city map of Jerusalem in the Appendix on page 130. You can read the Bible passages marked on the map and find the right places for each passage on the map.

Maundy Thursday

The night before the crucifixion of Jesus, he and his disciples ate together; he prayed alone in the garden of Gethsemane and Judas betrayed him.

Read Mark 14:12–52 together, which is the story of what happened on Maundy Thursday. Read John 13:2–12, which is the story of Jesus washing the disciples' feet. Put bread on a plate and wine (or red grape juice) in a glass. Place them beside a cross on a table or windowsill where you can see them and be reminded of Jesus' last supper with his disciples.

Wonder together about the following questions:

• Why are the events of Maundy Thursday important for us today?
• Why did Jesus wash the feet of his disciples?
• Why did the disciples let Jesus down?
• How do we let Jesus down?

A Maundy bag

Make a small drawstring bag to remind you of Judas' bag with its 30 pieces of silver, and of the British monarch distributing Maundy money. You could put a small gift in the Maundy bag and take it to someone who is ill or alone.

You could put a collection of new coins in the Maundy bags, one of each denomination. Place the bags on the supper table, one for each person present.

Today, the Queen follows a very old tradition of giving Maundy money to a group of pensioners. This tradition dates back to the reign of Edward I in the 13th century. Every year on Maundy Thursday the Queen attends a Royal Maundy Service in one of the many cathedrals throughout the United Kingdom. Maundy money is given to male and female pensioners from local communities near the cathedral where the service takes place. The same number of men and women receive the Maundy money as the Queen's age.

Foot washing

Remember Jesus washing the feet of the disciples by washing each other's feet or hands.

Passover meal

The first Passover is described in the Bible in the book of Exodus, chapter 12. It took place when the Israelites were still slaves in Egypt. One lamb was killed for each Israelite household and the blood was painted on the doorposts. This would be a sign to the 'angel of death' to 'pass over' the house and not kill the oldest boy in the family. The family were to eat the lamb, bitter herbs and unleavened bread (flat bread that has no yeast) before they left Egypt that night to go to the promised land.

God said that every year the children of Israel should celebrate this festival to remember the night when they were saved from slavery in Egypt. This is the festival that Jesus and his disciples were celebrating at the Last Supper.

The Passover meal was a special family occasion and can be adapted for your family, as follows.

You will need:
- A joint of lamb, roasted with garlic and herbs
- A small bowl of horseradish sauce
- A small bowl of salt water
- A small bowl of haroseth (date paste) or apple sauce
- A matzo cracker or pitta bread
- Wine or grape juice
- A large white candle

Instead of roast lamb, vegetarians might have a nut roast with herb stuffing.

Place all the items on the table and light the candle. Read out the following traditional questions and answers for this meal time.

Question: Why do we have bitter herbs (horseradish sauce) to eat today?

Answer: The bitter herbs remind us of the bitterness of slavery. They remind us of when God's people were slaves in Egypt long, long ago.

Question: Why is there salt water to taste today?

Answer: The salt water reminds us of the tears God's people cried when they were slaves in Egypt.

Question: Why have we got this haroseth paste today?

Answer: This sauce reminds us of the mud that God's people had to use to make bricks when they were slaves in Egypt.

Question: Why have we got lamb to eat today?

Answer: The lamb reminds us of the lamb's blood that protected the houses of God's people in Egypt, so that the angel of death passed over them and didn't hurt their eldest sons. It also reminds us that Jesus is the Lamb of God who died for us on Good Friday so that we could be friends with God.

Question: Why have we got flat bread to eat today?

Answer: The bread reminds us of the way God rescued his people from Egypt. They had to leave in such a hurry that there was no time for the bread to rise. It also reminds us that Jesus took bread at his Passover meal and gave it to his friends saying, 'Eat this; this is my body given for you. Do this to remember me.'

Question: Why do we drink wine today?

Answer: The wine reminds us of God's blessing, when he rescued his people from Egypt and took them to a land full of good things. It also reminds us that at the Passover meal Jesus took a cup of wine and said, 'This is my blood, poured out for you. Do this to remember me.'

As people taste the foods in turn, choose from the words:

- Like
- Don't like
- Don't mind

Alternatively, you could have a written list and place a tick, cross or question mark next to each item.

Finally, someone says, 'We eat this food today to remember God's rescue of his people at Passover and at Easter time, and the way he still guides us today. Let's give thanks to God together.'

Good Friday story

Jesus allowed himself to be put to death. The story of Good Friday is central to the Christian faith but can be very difficult to share with children. Try to find ways of doing this which are appropriate to your family.

Read about what happened in:

- Matthew 26:57—27:61
- Mark 14:53—15:47
- Luke 22:54—23:56
- John 18:28—19:42

Make or buy hot cross buns and eat them together.

Wonder together about the following questions:

- Why did Jesus' crucifixion happen?
- Did it have to happen?
- Were the people afraid of goodness, of new ideas, or what?
- Did people behave differently because they were part of a crowd?
- Why did the religious leaders behave the way they did?
- What would we have done if we had been there?
- What are the implications for us today?

Look at the cress you sowed on Palm Sunday. Has it grown into a green hill yet?

Cross of twigs

Collect some pieces of twig and make them into a cross using string or yarn. Put the cross where you can see it, to be reminded of what happened on Good Friday.

Use flexible twigs to make a crown of thorns. It could be hung above the cross you have made.

Place cards

Make place cards in the shape of a cross for each member of the family. Use them at family meals on Good Friday.

Good Friday prayers

Collect pictures, headlines and short articles from newspapers and magazines about pain, suffering and loss. Make them into a cross shape and use them as a focus for prayer.

Remember to put a cross in the window and try to have quiet family prayers at 12 noon and 3 pm, the traditional time of the crucifixion.

Good Friday rhyme

The rhyme on the following page originated in Mozambique. Here are some actions that you could use with it:

- Tree: stretch arms out sideways, shoulder high
- World: make a circle with arms
- Nest: cup hands
- Bird: wave hands and arms like wings
- Sky: move outstretched arm along skyline
- Clouds: make circles in the air with index finger
- Rain: move hands up and down
- Ground: touch floor with hands
- Corn: put one elbow to the floor with forearm upright
- Man: touch chest with hands
- Cross: make the sign of the cross with arms out in front of yourself

This is the tree which grows in the world for all of us,
which God made.

This is the nest which is in the tree,
which grows in the world for all of us,
which God made.

This is the bird which built the nest,
which is in the tree,
which grows in the world for all of us,
which God made.

This is the sky where flies the bird,
which built the nest,
which is in the tree,
which grows in the world for all of us,
which God made.

These are the clouds which float in the sky,
where flies the bird,
which built the nest,
which is in the tree,
which grows in the world for all of us,
which God made.

This is the rain which comes from the clouds,
which float in the sky,
where flies the bird,
which built the nest,
which is in the tree,
which grows in the world for all of us,
which God made.

This is the ground where falls the rain,
which comes from the clouds,
which float in the sky,
where flies the bird,
which built the nest,
which is in the tree,
which grows in the world for all of us,
which God made.

This is the corn which grows in the ground,
where falls the rain,
which comes from the clouds,
which float in the sky,
where flies the bird,
which built the nest,
which is in the tree,
which grows in the world for all of us,
which God made.

This is the man who cuts the corn,
which grows in the ground,
where falls the rain,
which comes from the clouds,
which float in the sky,
where flies the bird,
which built the nest,
which is in the tree,
which grows in the world for all of us,
which God made.

This is the cross where Jesus died
to save the man who cuts the corn,
which grows in the ground,
where falls the rain,

which comes from the clouds,
which float in the sky,
where flies the bird,
which built the nest,
which is in the tree,
which grows in the world for all of us,
which God made.

Celebrating Holy Saturday

On this day, we look back with regret but look forward in anticipation, so it is a day of waiting and of preparation.

Read about Joseph and Nicodemus putting Jesus' body in the tomb in John 19:38–42. Read about the women preparing and waiting in Luke 23:54–56.

You might like to make a Simnel cake (see the recipe on page 26) and decorate it with eleven balls of marzipan for the 'faithful' disciples. You could include an Easter chick in the decorations.

If you have not already done so, seal the tomb in your Easter garden. Perhaps you could collect a bare branch or twig and put it in a large pot ready to make an Easter tree tomorrow. Alternatively, set up an Easter egg hunt for Easter morning, but keep it as a surprise for the children.

A paschal candle

You will need:
A thick candle (white or cream); five coloured mapping pins; decorations such as stick-on stars or transfers

Stick the mapping pins into the candle to make a cross shape. Put the top pin approximately one-third of the way down the candle, so that the candle can safely stay lit throughout your meal. Then add the decorations.

If you are more adventurous, carefully carve a design into the candle and then add colour with melted wax crayons. This will need considerable care, as heating the wax crayons can become extremely messy, but the finished candle is very effective.

Put the paschal candle in a bowl of sand and surround it with other candles. In the dark, light the paschal candle and then light the others from it.

Wonder together about the following questions:

- How do you feel about this day?
- What is good about having to wait?
- Has preparing for Easter Day made you think more about what it means?
- How important is the experience of sadness to our understanding of joy?

✛

Celebrating Easter and Ascension at home

The Easter Day story

Today we rejoice in the resurrection of Jesus, which is central to the Christian message. Easter is the oldest and most important Christian festival. For Christians, the dawn of Easter Sunday, with its message of new life, is the high point of the Christian year. If Jesus hadn't risen from the dead, Christianity wouldn't have started and there would be no Christianity as we know it today.

Read together the story of Easter Day. Each of the Gospels emphasises the appearance of the risen Jesus to different people.

- Matthew 28:1–10
- Mark 16:1–8
- Luke 24:1–43
- John 20:1–29; 21:1–19

Go to church today. Roll away the stone from the tomb of the Easter garden and add flowers to the garden. Light the paschal candle as the centrepiece for all your meals today.

Easter eggs

Have an Easter egg hunt. Decorate boiled eggs for breakfast. Cut the cress on your 'green hill' and make egg and cress sandwiches for lunch or tea. Hang decorated eggs on the Easter tree branch that you collected yesterday.

Bread dough chicks

You will need some readymade bread dough and some raisins. Form some of the bread dough into little buns. On each one, pinch out a beak shape and poke raisins in for eyes. Cook the dough, following the instructions on the packet. When cool, decorate the chicks with ribbons.

Easter nests

Make Easter nests from cornflakes or other cereal, dipped in melted chocolate, and fill them with tiny eggs.

Easter grace

Say grace before lunch. One person could say, 'Alleluia, the Lord is risen.' Everyone could then reply, 'Alleluia, he is risen indeed.'
Wonder together about the following questions:

• What is it about Easter that makes it even more important than Christmas?
• What stories are there in your family that speak of new life?

Five prayer stations for Easter

You can use just one of these stations or scatter several through the house or garden if you have space. Print out the suggested prayer activities for each station.

Butterflies: hope

Place some fabric butterflies on a table alongside a picture of a chrysalis.

> Butterflies are a sign of new life, freedom and hope. Pick up and hold a butterfly and think of a situation that needs to find the hope of Jesus' new life. Place the butterfly back down carefully as you say 'Amen' to your silent prayer.

Chrysalis: memories

Place some large stones next to a picture of a chrysalis with some blank sticky notes or squares of paper.

> As you look at the chrysalis, which looks so lifeless, think about some situations in your life or the world that seem hard and difficult and are waiting for change. Pick up a blank piece of paper and place it under or on the stones as a sign of your prayer that God will ease the situation.

Eggs: promise

Place a bowl of eggs and a bowl of mini-eggs next to each other, with enough mini-eggs for everyone taking part. (Remember to offer an alternative for anyone who can't eat chocolate.)

> Eggs are great things! Sometimes they contain the promise of new life; sometimes they are simply a good basic food. As you look at the eggs, give thanks to God for his promises for us and for the world. Take a mini-egg and, as you eat it, pray for peace and justice throughout the world.

Daffodils: joy

Place a large bunch of daffodils in a bright vase, together with a large empty plate, some crayons or pencils and some sticky notes or slips of paper.

> It's hard to look at daffodils and feel sad! The bright colour makes us feel joyful. As you look at them, give thanks to God for all that brings you joy today. Pick up a paper slip, draw a smiley face on it and place it on the plate as a sign of your thanks.

Easter garden: good news

Display an Easter garden with a tomb and rolled-away stone.

> Take a moment to look at the garden. Pray that the good news that Jesus is alive will be real in your life today. Touch the rolled-away stone as a sign of your belief and trust in Jesus.

Celebrating Ascension

At Ascension we remember Jesus leaving his disciples to become one with God. The risen Jesus is no longer bound to earth's space and time.

Read Luke 24:45–53 together. In this passage, Jesus tells his disciples to wait in Jerusalem until the promised Holy Spirit comes. Read Acts 1:1–11 together. In this passage, Jesus entrusts his mission to his disciples and then leaves them.

Any of the following activities might be good ways of celebrating Ascension together.

- Make and wear crowns from gold paper or card.
- Take a picnic to a high place and enjoy the view, too.

- Go for a walk in pairs. One person wears a blindfold while the other directs or leads them around an obstacle course.
- Write a letter to a friend or relative who lives a long way away.
- If you enjoy singing as a family, sing 'Jesus' love is very wonderful' together and do the actions.

Wonder together about the following questions.

- Why does the Ascension matter?
- What difference does it make to us?
- How can we be God's witnesses (see Acts 1:8)?
- The symbol for the ascension is a crown. What sort of king was Jesus when he lived on earth? Is he any different now?

✠

Creative ideas for Easter crafts

A gift-filled home

You will need:
A house shape copied on to thin card (see template on page 131); scissors and glue; colouring pens and pencils

This is a suitable craft for Mothering Sunday.

Talk with the children about the ups and downs of family life as they fold and glue their shapes together. Suggest that they make the houses look like their own homes by drawing windows and doors and adding members of their own family on the outside or looking through the windows. On the roof, they could write a special 'thank you' message to their mother or carer, and pop a tiny gift inside.

Donkey hobby horse

You will need:
A brush or broom end; plastic carrier bag; white, brown or grey paper or fabric; thin card; wool, string or sticky tape

Cover a brush or broom end with a plastic carrier bag and then cover again with white, brown or grey paper or fabric. Secure by tying with wool, string or sticky tape.

Turn the brush sideways and stick on ears at the sides, using the same paper or fabric as for the head, backed on to card.

Cut out card circles for eyes and stick them on to the sides, in front of the ears.

Hens and chicks

You will need:
A paper plate; paintbrushes; orange, red and yellow paint; triangles of brightly coloured paper; thin strips of orange, red and yellow tissue paper, about 15 cm long; circles of black paper; glue and scissors

Fold the paper plate in half and open it out, to form a crease. Paint the back of the plate in shades of orange, red and yellow paint. Fold the plate in half again, along the crease.

For a beak, cut out a triangle of red or orange paper and glue it on at one end of the fold. Cut out circles for the eyes and stick them on either side of the plate, near the beak. Glue other triangles of paper to the top of the fold and, perhaps, around the eyes. Gather the tissue paper strips into a bunch and twist them together, then stick them on for a tail.

When placed on its open edges, the hen will rock back and forwards as though 'pecking'.

Chicks can be made by drawing around a saucer on a piece of card, cutting it out, folding and decorating as above.

Draw an Easter bunny

Draw an egg shape for the head and a bigger one underneath for the body. Draw two ears and draw lines inside the ears, too. Draw two feet below the bunny's body and add a tail. Draw in two eyes, a nose and curved mouth and add some whiskers. Colour however you like.

Potato printed chicks

You will need:
Potatoes cut in half; bright orange paper; orange and yellow paint; glue and scissors; black felt-tip pen; backing paper, painted green and blue for grass and sky

Protect your surfaces. Then pour the paint into dishes big enough for the potato to fit in. Dip the flat side of the potato into the paint and press it firmly on to the backing paper for the body of the chick.

Cut a triangle of bright orange paper and glue it on to the side of the body for a beak. When the paint is dry, add an eye, wings, a tail and some feet with a black felt-tip pen.

Spring flower prints

You will need:
Potatoes and hard pears cut in half; yellow and green paint; a bottle top; backing paper

Protect your surfaces. Then pour the paint into dishes big enough to take the potato and pear. Dip the flat side of the pear into the yellow paint and press it firmly on to the backing paper, then lift it off. Place a bottle top at the pointed end of the shape you have printed. Print more pear shapes around the bottle top. Lift off the bottle top. Dip a finger into the green paint and print dots in the middle of the pear prints to make the centre of the flower.

For leaves, dip the flat side of a potato into the green paint and press around the flower. You could paint a flower stem using the green paint.

You could make different flowers by cutting shapes into potato halves and using different coloured paints.

Surprise eggs

You will need:
A cardboard egg box and six eggs; paint and brushes; scissors; crayons; food dye; small gifts (such as wrapped mini-eggs, small chicks and so on); a length of ribbon long enough to go around the egg box

Protect your surfaces and give children aprons to wear.

Trim off any rough bits from the egg box. Paint the inside of the egg box in a bright colour, turn it upside down and paint the outside. Leave it to dry.

Tap the pointed end of an egg with a spoon to crack the shell. Pull off the pieces of broken shell and tip out the insides into a bowl. Do the same with all six eggs. (You could make scrambled egg with the insides.) Wash the empty shells and leave them upside down to dry.

Use crayons or food dyes to decorate the eggs: take care, as they will be fragile.

Put a tiny Easter gift inside each egg and place the eggs, upside down, into the egg carton. Close the egg box and tie a ribbon around it. You could also decorate the box by cutting out butterflies or flowers and sticking them on.

Cress egg-heads

You will need:
An egg; cotton wool; mustard and cress seeds; card pieces (such as postcards); card and paper scraps; crayons; glue; stapler; scissors

Tap the pointed end of an egg with a spoon to crack the shell. Pull off the pieces of broken shell and tip out the insides into a bowl. Wash out the empty shell.

Fill the eggshell with cotton wool and pour in water (perhaps using a spoon). Tip the egg so that any excess water drains out. Put the egg into an egg carton and sprinkle mustard and/or cress seeds over the top.

Leave the egg in a light place and add a little water every day. The seeds will grow in about a week.

Cut a narrow strip of card, about 8 cm long and 2 cm wide. Bend it around and staple the ends together. Stand the egg on top of the cardboard ring. Add a face to the egg with crayons or scraps of paper.

Knitted chicks

You will need:
- Small amounts of double knitting yarn in chick colours (yellow, orange, beige)
- Oddments of double knitting yarn in black and dark orange or red
- Pair of 3 mm (No. 11) knitting needles
- Small amount of washable toy stuffing

Body

- Cast on 10sts for lower edge and p1 row.
- 1st inc row: inc knitwise in each st – 20sts. P1 row.
- 2nd inc row: (inc in next st, k1) to end – 30sts. Ss 3 rows.
- 3rd inc row: (inc in next st, k2) to end – 40sts. Ss 11 rows.
- 1st dec row: (k2, k2tog) to end – 30sts. Ss 5 rows.
- 2nd dec row: (k1, k2tog) to end – 20sts. P1 row.
- 3rd dec row: (k2tog) to end – 10sts.
- Break off yarn, thread end through remaining sts, pull up tightly and secure.
- Gather cast on edge, pull up tightly and secure.
- Join row ends together, leaving an opening. Stuff firmly and close opening.

Beak

- Using dark orange or red yarn, cast on 2sts. P1 row.
- Inc row: inc kwise in first st, k1 – 3sts. P1 row.
- Dec row: k1, k2tog – 2sts.
- P2tog and fasten off.
- Fold beak in half widthways and join tiny row ends together. Pin folded edge vertically to centre front of head just below first dec row and sew in position.
- With black yarn, embroider eyes either side of beak.

Wings (make two)

- Cast on 4sts. P1 row.
- 1st inc row: inc kwise in first st, k to last 2sts, inc kwise in next st, kw.
- P1 row. Repeat last 2 rows once more. 8sts.
- Dec 1st at each end of next row and 2 following alternate rows – 2sts.
- P1 row. K2tog and fasten off.
- Position wings at sides of body and sew in place.

Abbreviations

K	knit
P	purl
St	stitch
Tog	together
Dec	decrease (by taking 2 stitches together)
Inc	increase (by working twice in same stitch)
Ss	stocking stitch (knit on right side, purl on wrong side)

Jesus ascends to heaven

You will need:
A paper cup; blue and white paint or paper; a copy of the figure of
Jesus and the cloud printed on to thin card (see template on page
132); a length of white string or yarn; scissors; sticky tape

Copy and cut out the Jesus figure and cloud. This can be coloured
in by the children if they wish. Paint the paper cup blue and paint
on some white clouds to look like sky, or cover it with paper
instead. Make a hole in the bottom of the cup.

Tape one end of the white string to the bottom of the cloud and
thread the other end down through the hole in the bottom of the
upturned cup. Tape the free end of the string to the top of Jesus'
head.

Now, if you pick up the cup and pull the cloud upwards, Jesus
will disappear into the sky.

You could write on the cloud, 'I will be with you always', which
you can read in Matthew 28:20.

✤

Creative ideas for the local community

Palm Sunday parade

A parade is a very visual witness and it can be as simple or as complicated as you feel able to make it. If you can find a real donkey to lead the parade, it will add to the atmosphere. Otherwise the children could make hobby horse donkeys (see page 82), which are great fun.

If you have a stock of costumes from your nativity play, the children could dress up in them to represent the crowd of people who were there when Jesus arrived in Jerusalem. Make sure you have enough palm crosses for everyone, too.

You will need to organise your route and, if you are using roads, you may need to inform the police for safety reasons. Decide where you are going to stop on the route and, if necessary, warn the people in the vicinity of what is happening.

Decide how you are going to divide up the Palm Sunday story and which songs and prayers to use. Ask different people to read, too. Ensure you have enough copies of song and prayer words for everyone so that they feel included.

It is a good idea to have the last stop of your parade at your church so that refreshments can be available. These could be very simple but, if your parade is in the morning, you could have lunch together. Don't forget to advertise your parade well!

Your imagination is the limit. Your parade could be a really short and simple one—for example, from the church lychgate to the church hall, then to the church entrance and finally up to the altar. Alternatively, you could walk around your town or village, stopping at a variety of places along your way.

Prayer stations

Before the parade, create six stations in the church, with the following objects:

- A plate of pitta bread, some wine or red grape juice in a jug, and paper cups.
- A bag of silver coins.
- Something to represent Roman soldiers (for example, a helmet, sword or picture of an army).
- A bowl of water.
- A wooden mallet and some big nails (perhaps a crown of thorns as well).
- Some myrrh or other oil, and strips of cotton or muslin.

Set up a sign for each station: The Last Supper, Betrayed, Arrested, Condemned, Crucified and Buried.

Parade liturgy

For the parade you will need palm crosses and copies of the words of the prayers and songs.

As people arrive, invite them to choose their palm cross. Make sure everyone has sight of any words required.

Read aloud:

Today is Palm Sunday when we remember Jesus' triumphant entry into Jerusalem. Like him, today we will be taking the Easter story out into the streets. It was a great day for shouting praises to Jesus. For a few moments, everyone thought he was the king they were expecting, but then the crowds drifted away and the disappointment set in. People began to moan and grumble because nothing seemed to change. They hadn't understood what was going to happen. They hadn't understood just how big the plan was: Jesus is the Saviour of the world!

We forget, too. We shout and sing, but too often our praises turn to grumbles. Let's stand in silence and look at the palm cross for a moment.

Lord God, it's easy to wave the cross in praise but hard to give you thanks every day. Forgive us our selfishness and greed.
Lord, have mercy.
Lord, have mercy.

Lord God, it's easy to hold a palm cross, but we forget that Jesus is the Saviour of the world. Forgive us our laziness and neglect.
Christ, have mercy.
Christ, have mercy.

It's easy to have a cross for a day, but we forget that we are called to take up our cross every day. Forgive us for going our own way.
Lord, have mercy.
Lord, have mercy.

May almighty God bring us his pardon and peace, now and for ever.
Amen

Song suggestion: 'We have a king who rides a donkey'

Process to first stop. Read aloud:

Jerusalem was full of Jewish pilgrims waiting to celebrate Passover. The place was busier than Oxford Street on Christmas Eve. Jesus was famous and everyone wanted to see him. They cheered and shouted as the king of the Jews, the Saviour, arrived in the city. Some expected him to come on a warrior's charger like a conquering hero, but Jesus arrived on a humble donkey. The crowds went wild! They waved palm leaves and made a carpet of their cloaks down the main street.

Encourage cheering and waving of palms, and flags and banners if you have them. Read aloud:

Jesus and his friends had arrived in Jerusalem. Their first question was, 'Where are we going to celebrate Passover?' The powerful religious leaders had a different question. 'This Jesus is a troublemaker. How can we get rid of him?'

Song suggestion: 'Make way, make way'

Pray aloud:

Lord God, thank you for the stories you told, the things you did, the words you said. Help us, your church, to remember all that your life and death mean, and to live our lives serving other people. ***Amen***

Process to second stop. Read aloud:

When Jesus entered Jerusalem, he was treated like a celebrity. The people cheered and laid down palm leaves to cover his path. This was their equivalent of laying down the red carpet for him. If Jesus came here today, would we give him the red carpet treatment? What would we lay down for him to walk on?

92

Would it be a coat or scarf? Would it be a bag or a hat? If it was red, so much the better for making a red carpet, but it could be anything of any colour that you would willingly lay down.

Living Lord, what will we give you? Will we lay out the red carpet for you? What will we lay down before you as you walk into our lives?

Pause.

Come, Lord Jesus.
Amen

Song suggestion: 'Give me joy in my heart'

Process to the church. Read aloud:

Palm Sunday is the start of Holy Week. During the week we will remember the events that led up to Jesus' death and his resurrection on Easter Day. Today we remind ourselves of what he suffered: this is called the story of his passion. Around the church are six stations marking stages in the passion story. There is a collection of objects for you to look at, feel, smell, listen to and even taste. Take some time to explore each station and to think about the things you find there. What story do they tell?

Leave at least ten minutes for people to explore the prayer stations.

Today we have taken the story of Palm Sunday out into the streets where we live, and we have done so for three reasons.

Firstly, we told the story outside because it is a story for everyone, not just for those of us inside this building. Secondly, we told the story outside because the story is as real for us today as it was nearly 2000 years ago. And thirdly, it is to remind ourselves that we are part of a crowd, too, and we can be as fickle as that crowd in Jerusalem. Jesus died because none of us is perfect. His death means that all of us can be forgiven.

As we move through Holy Week we will be telling parts of the story in more detail, and on Easter Sunday it will be time to tell the happy ending. For now, in a moment of quiet, let's remember what we have heard today.

Song suggestion: 'Ride on, ride on in majesty' or 'All glory, laud and honour'

Pray aloud:

Lord Jesus, Son of God, this week may we walk with you through the places of your passion. May we praise you with hosannas and remember that it is our sins that cry out, 'Crucify!' Make us witnesses of your sacrifice. *Amen*

You may like to finish with refreshments or share lunch together.

Passion play

The passion play on pages 96–102 can be planned and rehearsed well in advance or it can easily be organised in a day with a group of children. If using a cast of children, meet in the morning and spend a couple of hours explaining the play and going through the parts. Have a break for lunch and then invite people to come to a performance.

The main speaking parts are off-stage or to the side of your performance space, as the conversations are overheard, so lines do not need to be learnt. Pilate needs to learn his lines, however, and so do a few crowd members.

It works well if Caiaphas and the priests are not seen at the start, so that the first conversation comes as a surprise. They can be visible after that.

Jesus does not appear in person. The large cross could have a shadowy figure painted on it if required. This can be effective.

The 'Barabbas' scarves can be made by the children. Either cut out fabric letters spelling out 'Barabbas' and glue or sew them on, or use fabric paints to draw the name of Barabbas on the length of fabric. When folded at the neck, the fabric looks just like a scarf. When stretched and waved above the head, the name becomes visible.

Print a sheet for the audience, to include the crowd shouts and the words of the songs so that they can feel part of the crowd. The songs are only suggestions: anything suitable can be used.

Cast
Narrator; Caiaphas; Priest 1 and Priest 2; Pilate; four prayer readers. Non-speaking parts include soldiers, table setter, crowd and crowd leaders.

Props
Table with noisy money; bread and wine; large cross; crown of thorns; palms; lengths of fabric (like football scarves) with 'Barabbas' written on them; donkey (optional)

The cast and audience gather outside the venue.

Narrator: The time of the Passover festival was near, and Jesus and his disciples were on their way to Jerusalem. As they approached the city, Jesus sent two of his disciples, saying to them, 'Go to the village ahead of you, and at once you will find a donkey tied there, with her colt beside her. Untie them and bring them to me.' This took place to fulfil what was spoken through the prophet: 'Say to the daughter of Zion, "See, your King comes to you, gentle and riding on a donkey, on a colt, the foal of a donkey."'

The disciples went and did as Jesus had instructed them. They brought the donkey, placed their cloaks on it, and Jesus mounted. A very large crowd spread their cloaks on the road, while others cut branches from the trees and spread them on the road. The crowds that went ahead of him and those that followed shouted, 'Hosannah to the Son of David! Blessed is he who comes in the name of the Lord! Hosannah in the highest!'

While the Narrator is speaking, the children collect the donkey and process behind it towards the church, waving their palms. As they approach they sing the song 'Hosanna, hosanna'.

Crowd: Jesus! Jesus! Jesus is the King! (*clap, clap*)
Jesus! Jesus! Jesus is the King! (*clap, clap*)
Jesus! Jesus! Jesus is the King! (*clap, clap*)

Priest 1: My Lord.

Priest 2: My Lord high priest.

Caiaphas: Silence! What's all that noise?

Priest 1: It's Jesus, Sir.

Caiaphas: Jesus who?

Priest 1: Jesus of Nazareth.

Priest 2: The carpenter's son.

Caiaphas: Nazareth, huh! What good ever came from Nazareth?

Priest 1: They say he's the Messiah.

Priest 2: The Christ.

Priest 1: The son of God.

Priest 2: The son of David.

Priest 1: The promised king.

Priest 2: He'll set us free from Rome.

Caiaphas: Who says?

Priest 1: His followers.

Priest 2: The people.

Priest 1: The crowd.

Priest 2: Even the children are shouting it.

Caiaphas: Tell them to stop.

Priest 1: They won't stop.

Priest 2: They can't stop.

Caiaphas: Tell him to make them stop.

Priest 1: He says, if they keep quiet, the stones on the ground will start shouting.

Caiaphas: Huh!

Priest 2: What shall we do?

Caiaphas: We wait.

Song: 'Make way, make way'

The audience enters the venue and sits down.

Narrator: Then Jesus and his disciples went into the temple and began to drive out those who were buying and selling there.

The crowd enter and go to the stage area, milling about. A table and its contents are spilled on the floor.

Crowd: Hurrah!
Priest 1: Look! He's wrecking the temple.
Priest 2: He's attacking the staff.
Priest 1: He's stealing the money.
Crowd: Hurrah!
Priest 2: He's letting the animals run wild.
Priest 1: Pigeons everywhere.
Priest 2: Temple money all over the floor.
Crowd: Hurrah!
Priest 1: It's sacrilege.
Priest 2: It's an insult.
Caiaphas: Silence! What of the people? What are they doing?
Priest 1: They're loving it.
Priest 2: They're lapping it up.
Priest 1: They're hanging on his words.
Priest 2: They cheer when he appears.
Crowd: Hurrah!
Priest 1: They're pouring in.
Priest 2: Never seen so many people.
Caiaphas: Silence! *(Thoughtfully)* He's doing it on purpose. He must be. He's never done this before. He's making himself their king.

Priest 1:   He can't do that.

Priest 2:   What'll happen to us?

Priest 1:   We must stop him.

Priest 2:   We must arrest him.

Priest 1:   But they'll riot.

Priest 2:   They'll lynch us.

Priest 1:   Chaos!

Priest 2:   Bloodshed!

Priest 1:   What shall we do?

Caiaphas: We wait.

Song: 'Ride on, ride on in majesty'

During the song, the crowd go and sit at the edge of the stage area.

Narrator: On the first day of the Passover, Jesus sent two of his disciples to prepare the Passover meal for them. In the evening, while they were eating, Jesus took bread and said, 'This is my body, broken for you. Eat it to remember me. This wine is my blood, poured out for many. Drink it to remember me.'

While the Narrator is speaking, the table is set with a loaf of bread and a flagon of wine.

Priest 1:   (*Whispering*) Sir! We have a man here.

Caiaphas: Who?

Priest 2:   One of his friends, Judas.

Priest 1:   He'll lead us to him, to arrest him.

Caiaphas: Where?

Priest 2:   Outside the city.

Priest 1: By night.

Priest 2: Away from the crowds.

Priest 1: Tonight.

Caiaphas: How much?

Priest 2: He says he'll take fifty.

Priest 1: He might take forty.

Caiaphas: Thirty.

Priest 2: Thirty, then. *(Pause)*

Caiaphas: Done.

The table is cleared.

Narrator: As soon as Judas arrived at the place where Jesus was, he went up to him, said, 'Teacher', and kissed him. Then the soldiers arrested Jesus and took him to the high priest's house, where they questioned him all night. Early in the morning they took him to Pilate, the Roman governor.

Pilate: Who are you, man? A king? King of the Jews? You don't look like a king. What have you done? Why have they brought you to me?

    (Reading from a list) 'Healed the sick. Restored sight to the blind. Taught people to love one another.' Do they love you or hate you, your people? They want me to crucify you. Who are you, Jesus? Son of God or son of man?

    Why don't you answer me, Jesus? Don't you realise, I have power over you. I can set you free, or have you killed. Which is it to be?

Narrator: Then Pilate brought out Jesus to the crowd, with another man, Barabbas, a bandit.

Pilate crosses the stage.

Pilate: Look! Here is the man! Which of these do you want me to set free for you?

Priest 1: Shout for Jesus.

Priest 2: Shout for Barabbas.

Crowd: Jesus/Barabbas.

Priest 1: Jesus! Jesus! *(Continues calling but changes to 'Barabbas')*

Priest 2: Barabbas! Barabbas! *(Continues calling)*

Crowd: *(Waving scarves)* Barabbas! Barabbas! Barabbas!

Pilate: What do you want me to do with Jesus?

All: Crucify him! Crucify him! Crucify him!

Pilate: Why? What has he done?

All: Crucify him! Crucify him! Crucify him!

The soldiers bring in the cross and erect it.

Pilate: I find nothing wrong with this man.

All: Crucify! *(clap, clap, clap)*
Crucify! *(clap, clap, clap)*
Crucify! *(clap, clap, clap)*

Pilate: Silence! Take him! Crucify your king. I wash my hands of this man's blood.

Crowd: Hurrah! Crucify! *(clap, clap, clap)* Crucify! *(clap, clap, clap)*

The soldiers erect the cross and put a crown of thorns on the top. A strike on a cymbal or something similar quietens the crowd.

Narrator: Then the soldiers took Jesus and crucified him. His mother and the other women watched from a distance.

Song: 'My song is love unknown'

Lord Jesus, thank you for the love you brought into the world when you came to us as a newborn baby. Thank you for the love you shared as you lived among us, healing the sick. Thank you for the love you poured out for us as you died on the cross to save us. **Amen**

Lord Jesus, by your suffering and death on the cross you bore the sins of the whole world. You said sorry on behalf of us all so that we might be forgiven. Help us to turn from darkness to light and follow you in the perfect way of love. **Amen**

Lord Jesus, king of the universe,
Ride on in humble majesty.
Ride on through conflict and debate.
Ride on through sweaty prayer and betrayal of friends.
Ride on through mockery and unjust condemnation.
Ride on through cruel suffering and ignoble death.
Ride on to the empty tomb and your rising in triumph.
Ride on to raise up your church and renew the whole earth in your image.
Ride on, King Jesus! **Amen**

Narrator: When he was dead they took him down from the cross and laid him in a tomb.

Song: 'Lord of the dance'

Good Friday walk

Good Friday is one of the most significant days in the church calendar. Some churches see it as primarily a day of silent vigil, remembering the pain of Jesus' death and identifying with the sense of loss and confusion felt by the disciples. Others see it as a day to celebrate the victory of the cross.

On Good Friday we remember Jesus who visibly carried his cross through the streets of Jerusalem. Holding a walk of witness in the community can be a powerful symbol.

The size of your community will be important in determining the sort of walk you organise.

Before you start, set your objectives: are you trying to demonstrate a church presence, encourage people to think about Easter or pray for the neighbourhood? Prayerfully plan the walk with these thoughts in mind. Decide where you are going to stop along the route, and plan your prayers accordingly. Arrange for different people to read and pray. You might like to include a few songs or some drama. Perhaps you could give out a suitable Bible verse or Easter card with the local service times listed on it. It might be a good idea to give people some thoughts to meditate on during the walk, so that they have a focus as they move from place to place. Think about safety aspects, too, as you might need to organise stewards for the route.

Here is a simple programme that could be adapted to suit your community.

- **Meet at the church.** Read Mark 14:32–42 and pray that you will be faithful in witnessing for Jesus. Perhaps sing an appropriate song (the Taizé chant 'Watch and pray', for example) and spend a few moments in silent prayer, reflecting on Jesus in the garden of Gethsemane.
- **Walk to a doctor's surgery or pharmacy.** Read Mark 14:43–65. Thank God for the steadfast love of Jesus. Pray for those who care for others in the community.

- **Walk to a police station.** Read Mark 14:66—15:15. Remember that Jesus was arrested, tried and unjustly sentenced. Pray for justice in the world, for lawmakers and those who enforce the law, for prisoners and those who work with them.
- **Walk to a village green, park or open space.** Read Mark 15:16–41. Reflect on Jesus' death. Think of people who believe and those who don't. Pray for everyone who lives and works in the community.
- **Walk to a school or preschool.** Read Mark 15:42–47. Reflect on the love that Jesus showed to others. Pray for those who care for others, for schools, the education system and for children and young people generally.
- **Return to the church.** Close with a short act of worship and include prayers for any area of the community you might have missed. Read Romans 8:1–5 or 1 John 4:1–7 and end with a blessing.

You might like to share hot cross buns and drinks together before departing.

Rogationtide and beating the bounds

Rogation Sunday is another opportunity to organise a walk around your district. You could start at your place of worship and either return there for a meal or organise a picnic half way through your walk.

The fifth Sunday after Easter was originally called Rogation Sunday because of the words in the Prayer Book Gospel for the day: 'Whatever you ask the Father in my name, he will give to you.' The Latin for 'ask' is *rogare*, so people began to call the day Rogation Sunday.

By the 17th century, the old Roman festival of Terminalia or Boundaries had been adopted by the church and served a practical purpose. In the days before Ordnance Survey maps, there were not always clear lines of demarcation between parishes, especially where there were open field systems. During the procession, boys were 'bumped' on prominent marks and boundary stones, or rolled in briars and ditches, or thrown in the pond to ensure that they never forgot the boundaries. The Victorians made the event more civilised by beating objects rather than people, and put it into the context of a service and procession.

In the Western Church, processions to bless the crops and to include 'beating the bounds' developed from the old Roman rites of Robigalia (*robigo* is Latin for 'rust' or 'mould'), when prayers were offered for crops to be spared from mildew.

Today the emphasis has shifted. It remains a time for blessing young animals and the crops growing in fields and gardens, so it is an opportunity to remember the sowing of seed and the birth of young animals. People who live near the sea often go out in boats to bless the fish and fishermen too.

The underlying themes of Rogationtide are renewal and resurrection, as it remains part of the Easter season.

The three days between Rogation Sunday and Ascension Day are also called Rogation Days.

Organising a Rogation walk

First of all, you will need to decide on your route. If you are stopping near houses or on a farm or someone else's land, you will need to speak to the residents to check that they have no objection. Then ask for help with preparing the refreshments. Ask different people to take part in the service in the places where you stop. If your church has a banner, you might like to ask someone to carry it to lead your walk.

Arrange to finish the walk in a place where you can celebrate with refreshments.

A service suggestion is given on page 119.

Ascension Day party

Ascension Day is a wonderful excuse for a party. It may be one of the four major feast days of the Christian year (along with Christmas, Easter and Pentecost), but it is often completely overlooked. This is partly because it falls on a weekday but also perhaps because it is easily overshadowed by the fire and excitement of Pentecost that follows ten days later. It wasn't always so, and some older children's leaders at your church may well remember a time when Ascension Day even meant a day off school.

This festival marks the transitional moment between Jesus' 40 days of resurrection appearances and the coming of the Holy Spirit. Just as the annunciation is the prelude to the life and work of Jesus, the ascension is the prelude to the life and work of the Spirit through the church. It therefore opens the third act of God's wonderful rescue plan for the world that moves from creation, through redemption to sanctification. Acts 1 stands alongside Genesis 1 and the Christmas narratives as a starting point for each stage of the great story of salvation.

If you decide to have a party, make sure you plan well in advance and invite all the children you have contact with, as well as their friends. Choose and book your venue and gather your team together. Allocate tasks at the planning session.

During the service, tea can be put out for the children. If you are able to hold the service in a different space, it is a welcome surprise for the children to return to. Perhaps someone could make a cake in the shape of a hill.

The following is a sample timetable for a two-hour party starting at 4.30 in the afternoon.

3.30   Team arrives and sets up
4.30   Registration and arrival activities
4.40   Welcome, warm up, set the scene
5.00   Activities

5.35   Games
5.55   Service
6.10   Tea
6.30   Finish and clear up

Suggested arrival activities

- Decorate bags to put crafts in
- Make a rocket from a cardboard tube
- Follow a maze (find your way through the clouds to heaven)
- Do an Ascension wordsearch

Suggested crafts

- Jesus ascends to heaven (page 88)
- Tiramisu (page 36)
- Ascension flag
- Badges made using a badge machine
- Write a prayer on a balloon
- Heavenly jellies (page 37)

Suggested games

- Musical clouds (similar to Musical islands, but using large paper cloud shapes)
- Cloud relay (running from one end of your space to the other by stepping on paper cloud shapes)
- Team games involving balloons
- Bubble blowing and giant bubbles

Suggested songs

- 'Jesus is King of everything' (Tune: 'Here we go round the mulberry bush')

- 'We want to see Jesus lifted high'
- 'You are the King of glory'

Suggested service outline

- Set the scene from Acts 1
- Songs
- Prayer of confession
- Story about the ascension
- Prayer based on the great commission

Great commission prayer

Go	*(point forward with one arm and finger outstretched)*
into all the world	*(describe a tiny circle with your outstretched finger and then make the circle bigger and bigger)*
and share the good news	*(cup hands together and offer the 'contents' around to people on the left and right)*
with everybody, everywhere	*(rapidly point to everyone in the whole group and beyond).*

And I will be with you.
Just wait—stop in Jerusalem
until you receive the promise.

✝

Creative ideas for celebrating special saints

During the season of Lent and Easter there are several saints whose festival days are celebrated. Among these are most of the patron saints of the British Isles—David, Patrick and George. Only St Andrew of Scotland is celebrated at a different time of year. His feast is on 30 November.

St David's Day (1 March)

St David is the patron saint of Wales and we celebrate his feast day on 1 March.

David was born in Wales around the year AD520. David, or Dewi, was a saint of Pembrokeshire (Dyfed) on the western tip of Wales. There were so many Welsh religious leaders in the fifth and sixth centuries that this period became known as the 'Age of Saints'.

David is probably the most popular of the Welsh saints. According to a biography written about him in 1090, he was born into a noble family and his mother was called Non. She became a saint herself. He spent much of his life praying and going without food in order to concentrate on God. When he did eat, his diet was mostly of leeks and bread, and he drank only water. David founded twelve monasteries in South Wales, including Menevia (where St David's Cathedral stands today). He settled at Menevia and died there.

There is a story that grew up about David and a swarm of bees. One of the monks who worked with him was an Irishman called Domnoc. For many years, Domnoc's job was to look after the bees, until the day came when he had to return to Ireland. He said goodbye to the monks and then to the bees he had cared for, and headed for his boat.

But the bees were not going to let him go easily. Suddenly there was a huge buzzing sound in the air. Here was trouble! The bees had decided to go with him. Leaving the boat on the shore, Domnoc took the bees back to their hives, but no sooner had he returned to his boat than the air was filled once more with the yellow and black honey-makers. What was Domnoc to do?

David was visiting the monastery at the time and heard about what was happening. He knew just what to do and gave the bees as a present to Domnoc. Domnoc and his bees left in peace (at least, as much peace as sailing with a swarm of bees would allow).

It is said that all bees in Ireland are, even today, descended from Domnoc's bees.

In Wales and some other parts of the United Kingdom, you can see statues and crosses that have a Celtic design on them.

Have a look at this Celtic cross and the design on it. Can you trace the design with a finger? Where will you start? Where will you finish? Notice the way the lines weave over and under one another. Are there any loose ends? Is there a beginning? Is there an end?

The patterns are designed to help us think about God. God is eternal and has no beginning or end. As you trace the design with your finger, spend some time quietly praising God and thanking God for always being there.

The word 'Celt' comes from the Greek word *keltoi*, which means 'barbarians'. 'Celt' is a modern name that describes many of the tribes of people living in the Iron Age.

The daffodil is the national flower of Wales, so perhaps you could fill a vase with daffodils and leave it in a prominent place.

A fingerprint bee

You will need:
Yellow and black paint; background paper

Dip your thumb into the yellow paint and press hard on the paper to make the body of the bee. Dip your little finger into the black paint and gently dot on a head and stinger. Make a couple of small dots in the middle of the body for a stripe. Dip your index finger into the black paint and then wipe most of the paint off. Use this finger to stamp two wings above the body.

You could make fingerprint bees on cards or even decorate flowerpots with them.

A prayer

Father God, thank you for all the stories I have heard about people doing kind and generous things to help others. May stories like that be the ones told about me, too. **Amen**

St Patrick's Day (17 March)

St Patrick is the patron saint of Ireland and we celebrate his feast day on 17 March.

There are many stories about the patron saint of Ireland; some are true but some are legends which have grown up over the years.

Patrick was born between 390 and 414, possibly in modern Cumbria. His father was a town councillor called Calpurnius who was a deacon in his local church. When Patrick was 16, he was captured by Irish pirates, who took him to work on a farm in the west of Ireland. After the comfort of his home, it was a bit of a shock to Patrick to have to work as a shepherd. During this time Patrick got to know God as a friend and companion and developed his prayer life.

After some years, Patrick had a message from God in a dream saying, 'Your ship is ready,' so he travelled to the east coast of Ireland and set sail for Britain. He was ordained and returned to Ireland in about 435. He spent the rest of his life teaching, ordaining clergy and setting up religious houses for monks and nuns. He died on 17 March 461, which is why this is the day when we specially remember him.

There is a legend that Patrick drove all the snakes out of Ireland. The green lands of Ireland were plagued with snakes. The high king of Ireland was at his wits' end and everyone was angry. 'You must do something, Sire,' everyone said. 'I know,' replied the king, 'but I don't know what to do!'

Suddenly a tall man arrived at the court and hammered on the ground with his staff. 'Who are you?' asked the king.

'My name is Patrick and I have come to rid Ireland of snakes,' Patrick replied.

Everyone cheered, and even the king couldn't resist a smile. 'Then you are very welcome here,' said the king. 'But how are you going to drive the snakes away?'

'I shall use my staff and the power of prayer,' replied Patrick.

'But we've prayed to all our gods and we've still got snakes!' said the king.

'Ah!' said Patrick. 'I am not talking about your gods but the one true God I believe in, and I shall pray for his power and help.'

'Well, it's worth a try. If your God can help you drive out the snakes, then I and all my people will worship your God, too.'

Patrick left the palace and walked to the top of a cliff. The wild waters of the ocean foamed and seethed far below. Patrick raised his wooden staff above his head and brought it crashing down on the ground. His voice roared out on the wind as he commanded the snakes to go.

The people could hardly believe their eyes as a slithering mass of snakes crawled to the edge of the cliff and flung themselves into the raging waters below. They were so grateful that the king and all his subjects were baptised and no snakes have been seen in Ireland to this day.

The national emblem of Ireland is the shamrock. Patrick used the three-leaved shamrock to explain how the trinity of Father, Son and Holy Spirit could exist as separate parts of the same being. His followers started to wear the shamrock, too.

Shamrock badge

You could make a shamrock badge to wear on St Patrick's Day. Using the template on page 133, cut out shamrock shapes from green card. Write the words 'Father', 'Son' and 'Holy Spirit' on the three parts of the leaf as a reminder of Patrick's teaching about the Trinity. Laminate the badge and attach a pin securely to the back.

A famous prayer

This hymn was probably not written by Patrick but is called 'St Patrick's Breastplate':

Christ be with me, Christ within me,
Christ behind me, Christ before me,
Christ beside me, Christ to win me,
Christ to comfort and restore me.
Christ beneath me, Christ above me,
Christ in quiet, Christ in danger,
Christ in hearts of all that love me,
Christ in mouth of friend and stranger.

The Annunciation (25 March)

On 25 March we celebrate the annunciation of Jesus's birth to Mary. It is a day when we give thanks for Mary's decision to say 'yes' to God and to accept what he wanted her to do. Nine months from this date, we celebrate the birth of Jesus at Christmas.

Mary was a young girl who lived in Nazareth. She was engaged to a carpenter called Joseph. One day Mary was very surprised to find that she had a most unusual visitor—an angel. This was no ordinary angel, either, but the archangel Gabriel. 'Don't be afraid, Mary,' said Gabriel. 'God has chosen you and you will have a baby. This baby will be special, and you will call him Jesus. His kingdom will last for ever.'

'How can this be?' asked Mary. 'I'm not married yet.'

'He will be the Son of God,' replied Gabriel, 'because nothing is impossible with God.'

Mary bowed before the angel Gabriel and said she would obey God. When she got up, the angel had gone.

Perhaps you could put the figures of Mary and the angel from your Christmas crib in a special place today.

Annunciation greeting card puzzle

You will need:
An old Christmas card with a picture of the annunciation or of angels; a piece of card, the same size as the Christmas card; glue; scissors; felt-tip pens; pencil; ruler

Stick the picture on to the piece of card and write a greeting on the back.

Using the pencil, lightly draw the shapes you want to cut out to make a jigsaw puzzle. You might want squares or crazy shapes. Cut the card into pieces, carefully following the pencil lines. When you've done that, you can either do the puzzle yourself or put it in an envelope and send it to a friend or relative.

Angel cake

This cake isn't like the three-coloured, layered cakes you can buy in supermarkets. Angel cake is a light and airy sponge cake. Because it is so light and airy, people have nicknamed it 'the food of angels'.

You will need:
- 40 g plain flour
- 100 g caster sugar
- 4 egg whites
- Pinch of salt
- ½ tsp cream of tartar
- 2 drops vanilla essence
- 300 ml whipping cream, whipped
- 225 g raspberries (thawed and drained if frozen)
- 1 litre deep, fluted ring mould or angel cake tin, greased
- Piping bag with star nozzle

Set the oven to 190°C (375°F, Gas 5).

Sieve the flour with half the sugar three times and set aside. Whisk the egg whites with the salt and cream of tartar until they form soft peaks. Whisk in the vanilla essence and remaining sugar in batches, two tablespoons at a time, until the mixture stands in firm peaks. Fold in the flour and sugar mixture.

Spoon into the tin and bake for 30–35 minutes until springy to the touch.

Turn the cake, still in the tin, upside down on a wire rack and leave to cool completely before lifting the tin off. Cut the cake in half horizontally, and fill and decorate with whipped cream and raspberries. Serve immediately.

Wonder together about the following questions:

- Think about the times when people have been messengers (the meaning of the word 'angels') who have given you God's good news.
- In what ways do we say 'yes' to God's call?
- Would we need to change to answer God's call?

A prayer

Father God, help us to be ready to say 'yes' to your call, just like Mary did. **Amen**

St George's Day (23 April)

St George is the patron saint of England and we celebrate his day on 23 April.

George lived in Israel nearly 300 years after Jesus' lifetime. The Roman army was still strong and powerful and, as soon as he was old enough, George became a Roman soldier. He loved doing daring things and visiting new places.

On his travels, George heard about Jesus and decided to become a follower. Being a Christian helped George to be even more gallant. Then, one day in the year 303, the Roman Emperor Diocletian passed a law to say that no one was allowed to become a Christian. When George heard about this law, he took a deep breath. He had to make a choice. The first option was that he could remain in the Roman army, keep quiet about his faith and stop living as Jesus taught. The second was that he could leave the army and just keep quiet. The last was that he could try to do something about the law.

George chose the last option. Before he went to see the Roman Emperor, he gave away everything he owned. Deep down, he knew what was likely to happen to him. To ask the mighty Diocletian to change the law would lead to certain death.

On 23 April 304, George was killed because he had stood up for what he believed was right. His brave action has never been forgotten and the story has been passed down from parents to their children.

Nearly 1000 years later, during the Crusades, soldiers began creating stories about George. The story about how he killed the dragon and rescued the king's daughter grew up out of a book called *The Golden Legend*, which was written by the Archbishop of Genoa in about 1275.

In the story, a dragon made a nest by the water supply at Lydda, where George grew up. The dragon insisted that, if the people wanted water, they had to bring a sheep each day for him to eat. When all the sheep had been killed, a young girl was chosen by drawing lots. On the day the princess's name was drawn, George happened to be travelling through the town. He took on the dragon, fought it bravely and defended himself with his shield, which had the sign of the cross on it. George defeated the dragon, the princess was saved and the people decided to follow George's example and find out about the Christian faith.

George's symbol, a red cross on a white background, has become the design of the English flag.

A red rose for St George's Day

You will need:
Red tissue paper; a green pipe cleaner; sticky tape

Cut three strips of tissue paper, one 6 cm wide, one 5 cm wide and one 4 cm wide. Concertina-fold each strip so you have a roughly square shape, just as you would to make a chain of paper people. Draw a petal shape with a strip across the bottom touching each fold (see the template on page 134). Cut out the shape, taking care not to cut through the folds at the bottom. Unfold the strips.

Starting with the thinnest strip, wind the petals around the pipe cleaner and secure with sticky tape. When you have added all three strips, twist the pipe cleaner around the tissue to keep it in place. Carefully tease out the petals to make it look like a rose.

A prayer

Father God, help us to know what we believe in and always to stand up for what is right. **Amen**

Appendix 1: Rogation walk

Here are some suggested readings, prayers and responses for a Rogation walk service. Don't feel you need to use all the sections: choose those that are relevant for your area.

At the church before setting out

- Introduction and greeting

Grace, mercy and peace from God our Father and the Lord Jesus Christ be with you.
And also with you.

- Hymn

Jesus said, 'This is why I tell you not to be anxious about food and drink to keep you alive and about clothes to cover your body. Surely life is more than food, the body more than clothes. Look at the birds in the sky; they do not sow and reap and store in barns, yet your heavenly Father feeds them. Are you not worth more than the birds? Can anxious thought add a single day to your life? And why be anxious about clothes? Consider how the lilies grow in the fields; they do not work, they do not spin; yet I tell you, even Solomon in all his splendour was not attired like one of them. If that is how God clothes the grass in the fields, which is there today and tomorrow is thrown on the stove, will he not all the more clothe you? How little faith you have! Do not ask anxiously, "What are we to eat? What are we to drink? What shall we wear?" These are the things that occupy the minds

of the heathen, but your heavenly Father knows that you need them all. Set your mind on God's kingdom and his justice before everything else, and all the rest will come to you as well.'
BASED ON MATTHEW 6:25–33

Let us go forth in peace.
In the name of Christ. Amen

At the village green, or some central place

Unless the Lord builds the house, its builders labour in vain. Unless the Lord keeps watch over the city, the watchman stands guard in vain. In vain you rise early and go late to rest, toiling for the bread you eat; he supplies the needs of those he loves… How good and pleasant it is to live together as brothers and sisters in unity.
BASED ON PSALM 127:1–2; 134:1

Bless the Lord, all you of upright spirit:
bless the Lord, you that are holy and humble in heart;
bless the Father, the Son and the Holy Spirit:
sing his praise and exalt him for ever.

Heavenly Father, you make families live together in unity. Bless all who live and work in this village (town). May our homes be places where there is love and where you are always present as the unseen guest. May those who work with skills of hand and mind have sufficient health and strength to fulfil their daily tasks and receive the harvest of their labour. May our children grow up to see your hand in the beauty of creation. And in the wise ordering of our village (town) in all its doings, may we see an image of your heavenly kingdom. Through Jesus Christ our Lord.
Amen

May the blessing of God rest on this parish. May all who go forth come again in peace. May the children learn and keep the faith of Jesus Christ. May his blessing rest on [insert names]. In the name of the Father, Son and Holy Spirit. **Amen**

At a place of worship

Unless the Lord builds the house, its builders labour in vain. Unless the Lord keeps watch over the city, the watchman stands guard in vain. In vain you rise early and go late to rest, toiling for the bread you eat; he supplies the needs of those he loves... How good and pleasant it is to live together as brothers and sisters in unity.

BASED ON PSALM 127:1–2; 134:1

Bless the Lord, all you of upright spirit:
bless the Lord, you that are holy and humble in heart;
bless the Father, the Son and the Holy Spirit:
sing his praise and exalt him for ever.

Eternal God, we rejoice in your promise that as our days are, so shall our strength be; we thank you for this place of worship where all may come freely to meet you. May this house of prayer be blessed and may it be a place of healing and happiness for all who enter its doors, through Jesus Christ our Lord. **Amen**

God of all grace, we ask your blessing on the ministry here and those who lead the worship and visit in this neighbourhood. Strengthen them for their tasks and give them the joy of knowing that they are instruments in fulfilling your own purpose of ministering, in Jesus Christ our Lord. **Amen**

At a local business

Bless the Lord, all you works of the Lord:
sing his praise and exalt him for ever.
Bless the Lord, you heavens:
sing his praise and exalt him for ever.

God said: 'By the sweat of your face you shall eat bread until you return to the ground, for out of it you were taken; you are dust, and to dust you shall return.'
BASED ON GENESIS 3:19

For the world of work in all its diversity:
Hear us, good Lord.
For the industry and workplaces in this parish:
Hear us, good Lord.
For the right ordering of work in time of technological change:
Hear us, good Lord.
For all expanding industries and for the promise of new jobs:
Hear us, good Lord.
For small business and cooperatives:
Hear us, good Lord.
For local trade and commerce:
Hear us, good Lord.

Save us from all that holds us captive. Restore our vision, that our mouths shall be filled with laughter and our tongues with songs of joy.
Amen

At a garden, orchard or allotment

God also said, 'Throughout the earth I give you all plants that bear seed, and every tree that bears fruit with seed: they shall be yours for food. All green plants I give for food to the wild animals, to all the birds of the air, and to everything that creeps on the earth, every living creature.' So it was, and God saw all that he had made, and it was very good.

BASED ON GENESIS 1:29–31

O let the earth bless the Lord:
bless the Lord, you mountains and hills;
bless the Lord, all that grows in the ground:
sing his praise and exalt him for ever.

God, by your favour each of us may share in the cultivation of the land: give us also such skill and patience in digging and planting and sowing that fruit and vegetables may emerge to nourish our bodies, and flowers to gladden our eyes; through Jesus Christ our Lord. **Amen**

May God bless our fruit trees and plants, bushes, vegetables and flowers. May he give us patience, contentment and trust in himself; in the name of the Father, Son and Holy Spirit. **Amen**

At a school

Sing to the Lord a new song; sing to the Lord, all the earth. Sing to the Lord, praise his name; proclaim his salvation day after day. Declare his glory among the nations, his marvellous deeds among all peoples.

PSALM 96:1–3 (NIV)

Bless the Lord, for your ways are perfect.
Bless the Lord for showing us the Way.
Bless the Lord for the minds you gave us.
May we praise you for ever.

God bless this school and all who work within its walls—the students who learn, the teachers who teach and care for them, and also those who keep the school clean and provide meals and play. May all prosper and find a joy in learning through Jesus Christ our Lord. **Amen**

May the blessing of God be on this school and all who enter its doors. May the parents too find satisfaction and encouragement. This we ask in the name of the Father, Son and Holy Spirit. **Amen**

At a field of crops

You care for the earth and make it fruitful; you enrich it greatly; filling its great channels with rain. In this way you prepare the earth and provide grain for its people. You water its furrows, level its ridges, soften it with showers, and bless its growth. You crown the year with your good gifts; places where you have passed drip with plenty; the open pastures are lush and the hills wreathed in happiness; the meadows are clothed with sheep and the valleys decked with grain, so that with shouts of joy they break into song.

BASED ON PSALM 65:9–13

Bless the Lord, sun and moon.
Bless the Lord, you stars of heaven.
Bless the Lord, all rain and dew.
Sing his praise and exalt him for ever.

God, you have blessed our ploughing and our sowing. Protect, we pray, from storm and blight, the young crops in our fields; and grant that after work late and early, we may enjoy a prosperous harvest; through Jesus Christ our Lord. **Amen**

May the blessing of God be on this field and on all the crops of our countryside. May the soil be wholesome and the crops sound; in the name of the Father, Son and Holy Spirit. **Amen**

At a field where there is livestock

God said, 'Let the earth bring forth living creatures, according to their various kinds: cattle, creeping things, and wild animals, all according to their various kinds.' So it was; God made wild animals, cattle, and every creeping thing, all according to their various kinds; and he saw that it was good.

BASED ON GENESIS 1:24–25

Bless the Lord, all birds of the air.
Bless the Lord, you beasts and cattle.
Bless the Lord, all people on earth.
Sing his praise and exalt him for ever.

Lord our Creator, you surround all things living with your love, and promise to save both humans and beasts. Thank you for the companionship of animals and birds, without which we would have a great loneliness of spirit; through Jesus Christ our Lord. **Amen**

May the blessing of God be on our fields, pastures and meadows. May they remain in good heart, unspoiled, and be at the service of humans and animals. May God bless the cattle, the sheep and the horses. May God preserve them from disease and keep them in good condition; in the name of the Father, Son and Holy Spirit. **Amen**

At a nursing home or hospital

You who live in the shelter of the Most High, who abide in the shadow of the Almighty, will say to the Lord, 'My refuge and my fortress; my God, in whom I trust.' You will not fear the terror of the night, or the arrow that flies by day, or the pestilence that stalks in darkness, or the destruction that wastes at noonday. A thousand may fall at your side, ten thousand at your right hand, but it will not come near you.

BASED ON PSALM 91:1–2, 5–7

Bless the Lord, you angels of the Lord.
Bless the Lord, all you his hosts.
Bless the Lord, you waters above the heavens.
Sing his praise and exalt him for ever.

Eternal God, we rejoice in your promise that as our days are, so shall our strength be. We ask your help for all who are old and wearied with the burden of life. In your strength may they find courage and peace, and in their advancing years may they learn more of your love. Through Jesus Christ our Lord. **Amen**

God of all grace, we ask your blessing on the work of doctors, nurses and those who tend the sick and elderly, especially in this neighbourhood. Strengthen them for their tasks, and give them the joy of knowing that they are instruments in fulfilling your own purpose of healing, in Jesus Christ our Lord. **Amen**

Closing prayers

Bless the Lord, all you works of the Lord:
sing his praise and exalt him for ever.
Bless the Lord, you heavens:
sing his praise and exalt him for ever.

For those who work on land or sea

Almighty God, whose will it is that the earth and the sea should bear fruit in due season, bless the labours of those who work on land and sea. Grant us a good harvest and the grace always to rejoice in your fatherly care; through Jesus Christ your Son, our Lord. **Amen**

For those engaged in commerce and industry

Almighty God and Father, you have so ordered our life that we are dependent on one another. Prosper those engaged in commerce and industry and direct their minds and hands that they may rightly use your gifts in the service of others; through Jesus Christ, your Son, our Lord. **Amen**

Let us pray with confidence as our Saviour has taught us:

Our Father, who art in heaven,
hallowed be thy name,
thy kingdom come;
thy will be done;
on earth as it is in heaven.
Give us this day our daily bread.
And forgive us our trespasses,
as we forgive those who trespass against us.
And lead us not into temptation;
but deliver us from evil.
For thine is the kingdom,
the power and the glory,
for ever and ever. Amen

- The dismissal

- Hymn

May God the Father of our Lord Jesus Christ, who is the source of all goodness and growth, pour his blessing upon all things created, and upon you his children, that you may use them to his glory and the welfare of all peoples. And the blessing of God almighty, the Father, the Son, and the Holy Spirit, be among you and remain with you always. **Amen**

Appendix 2: Templates

Palm leaf prayers

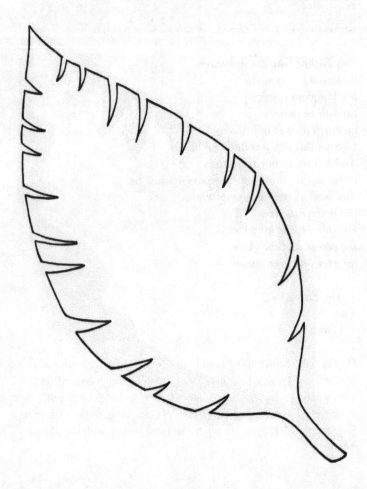

Easter box

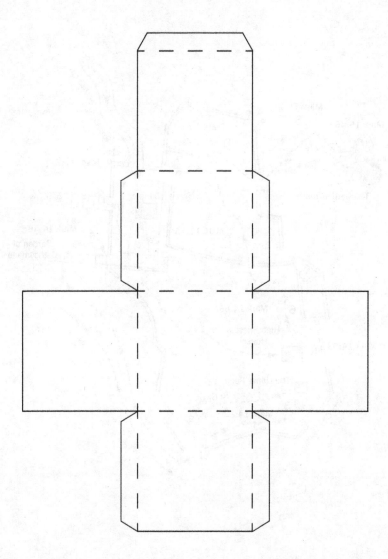

Jerusalem map

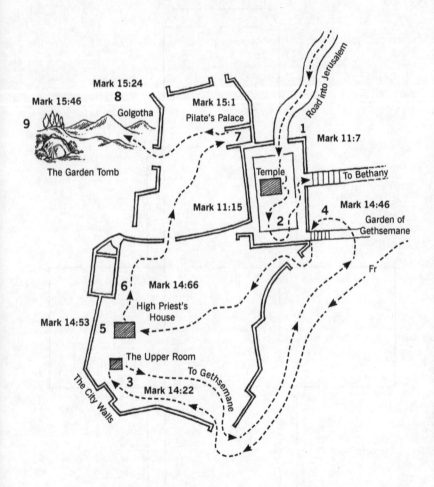

A gift-filled home

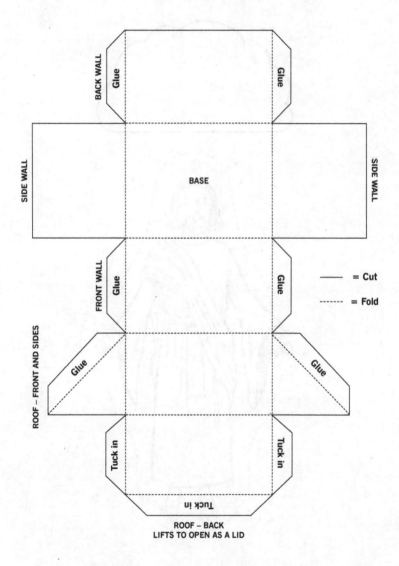

Jesus ascends to heaven

Shamrock

Red rose for St George's Day

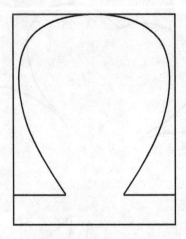

Index of activities

Creative Ideas for Advent and Christmas

80 seasonal activities for use with children

Creative Ideas for Advent and Christmas contains a wealth of inspirational easy-to-do ideas for the busy weeks in the lead-up to Christmas. All the ideas use readily available materials and have instant appeal. Many can be slotted into any situation, used to illustrate the story of Christmas, or just done for pure enjoyment as part of the exciting 'getting ready' time.

The activities are ideal for children aged 4–11, but will be enjoyed equally by people of all ages. There are 80 ideas in total, many of which could become part of traditional family, church and community celebrations each year.

Ideas include:
• Community events
• Recipes for easy Christmas cooking
• Creative ways to pray
• Christmas card crafts
• Simple decorations
• Fun-filled games

ISBN 978 1 84101 856 0   £8.99
Available from your local Christian bookshop or direct from BRF: please visit www.barnabasinchurches.org.uk.

Creative Ideas for All-Age Church

12 through-the-year programmes for informal church services and special one-off events

Karen Morrison

The twelve themes in this book contain a wealth of creative worship ideas, all designed to encourage the church family to listen to each other's stories. Through listening and worshipping together in a less formal setting, the material promotes creative thinking and enables people of all ages to learn together in worship and grow in faith as part of God's family.

Each theme includes introductory reflections on the season of the year; a biblical context; ideas for a visual display; age-specific activities; suggestions for sharing a meal; suggestions for reflections, prayers and sung worship and, finally, ideas for taking the theme further.

The themes can be used to plan stand-alone worship programmes or to follow the pattern of the Christian year.

ISBN 978 1 84101 663 4   £7.99
Available from your local Christian bookshop or direct from BRF: please visit www.barnabasinchurches.org.uk.

More Creative Mission

Over 40 further ideas to help church and community
celebrate special days and events throughout the year

Rona Orme

More Creative Mission contains an exciting mix of easy-to-run
outreach ideas for community-minded churches to use, whatever
the season or celebration and with groups of any size. Some of the
ideas follow the liturgical and seasonal calendar, while others can
be used at any time.

Alongside four special activity events—one for each season—
there is an extensive collection of fun and thought-provoking ideas
covering every month of the year. Some of the ideas are based
in church; some are for the church family to take into the wider
community or local schools and preschool groups; some involve
the wider community in the celebration of key events; others are
designed to promote social action by campaigning or fundraising
for specific needs within the community or overseas.

All the ideas are designed to appeal to children as well as adults,
but many can also be used if there are few or no children in the
church family.

ISBN 978 0 85746 148 3   £8.99
*Available from your local Christian bookshop or direct from BRF: please
visit www.barnabasinchurches.org.uk.*

Celebrating Festivals

Readings, reflections, crafts and prayer activities
for 20 major church festivals

Sally Welch

Ideal for use with all ages in church, Sunday school, midweek groups or activity days, this resource provides material for 20 major festivals throughout the church year.

Each section has a unifying theme and includes suggested Bible passages, a reflection for leaders, a Bible story retelling and questions, a prayer activity, 'messy' craft activities and edible craft activities. An additional dimension links each festival to a part of the church building, helping children to understand the idea of sacred space and explore the relationship between the physical and the spiritual.

The book also addresses the practicalities of crafting with children, with detailed advice on resources, setting up activities, recipes and safety.

ISBN 978 1 84101 711 2   £8.99
Available from your local Christian bookshop or direct from BRF: please visit www.barnabasinchurches.org.uk.

Edible Bible Crafts

64 delicious story-based craft ideas for children

Sally Welch

If you're looking for child-friendly Bible-themed cooking activities, this is the book for you!

Sally Welch brings the Bible to life for 3–11s with her range of edible crafts, covering twelve Old Testament stories, twelve New Testament stories and eight key festivals from the church year. Each unit gives the Bible story in a children's version, a short reflection on the passage, and a sweet and a savoury recipe idea.

The recipes use readily available ingredients and equipment, require no cooking during the craft session and can be used in a variety of situations, including Sunday schools, midweek clubs and Messy Church events.

The book also includes detailed information about set-up and preparation, tips on where to buy ingredients, and basic recipes to form the basis of the crafts, such as fairy cakes, biscuits and pastry, together with egg- and gluten-free alternatives.

ISBN 978 0 85746 243 5   £11.99

Available from your local Christian bookshop or direct from BRF: please visit www.barnabasinchurches.org.uk.

Enjoyed

this book?

Write a review—we'd love to hear what you think.
Email: reviews@brf.org.uk

Keep up to date—receive details of our new books as they happen.
Sign up for email news and select your interest groups at:
www.brfonline.org.uk/findoutmore/

Follow us on Twitter @brfonline

By post—to receive new title information by post (UK only), complete
the form below and post to: BRF Mailing Lists, 15 The Chambers, Vineyard,
Abingdon, Oxfordshire, OX14 3FE

Your Details
Name _____
Address _____
_____
Town/City _____ Post Code _____
Email _____

Your Interest Groups (*Please tick as appropriate)

- ☐ Advent/Lent
- ☐ Bible Reading & Study
- ☐ Children's Books
- ☐ Discipleship
- ☐ Leadership

- ☐ Messy Church
- ☐ Pastoral
- ☐ Prayer & Spirituality
- ☐ Resources for Children's Church
- ☐ Resources for Schools

Support your local bookshop
Ask about their new title information schemes.